A BRIDGE TO THE LIGHT

A BRIDGE TO THE LIGHT

By Pauline H. Firks

Born in East London, Pauline originally studied classical ballet and had a career in film, TV and theatre. Pauline then went on to become a reflexologist and a registered healer and now works as a public demonstration medium.

A Bridge to the Light *is the story of Pauline's journey to becoming a medium. It is in small part autobiographical and takes the reader through her various spiritual experiences and amusing stories.*

For over forty years, Pauline and her husband Terry have done voluntary cat rescue and proceeds from the sale of this book go towards animal rescue.

The knowledge and information contained in this book is the direct result of Pauline's work with spirit.

British Library Cataloguing-in-Publication data
A catalogue record for this book is available from the British Library

ISBN 978-1-5272-6955-2

Typeset by Carnegie Scotforth Books

Printed and bound by Halstan

CONTENTS

I would like to thank my dear husband, Terry,
for his invaluable help and contribution
in the creation of this book.

I dedicate this book to my beloved mother,
Vera Davis, in recognition of her amazing
compassion and dedication to animal rescue,
both in this country and Spain
and also to my beloved father, Ron Davis,
who guided me on my spiritual pathway.

CHAPTER ONE

How the Journey Began – The Story so Far

As a child of eleven, I remember going on holiday with my parents to Cornwall and having my first out-of-body experience. At the time it was very frightening as I didn't know what was happening to me. I had switched to an altered state of consciousness and I said to my father, 'Am I really here?' This was a very vivid and terrifying experience to me at the time and I only learnt more recently that one of my spirit guides, a French Sister of Mercy (a nun) named Celestine, drew very close to me too soon and was eager to work with me. In spirit, they find it very difficult to measure time, as they do not have twenty four hours a day or seven days a week – but all eternity. Due to this very powerful energy, I had this out-of-body experience and it must have brought me closer to the vibration of the spirit world, which exists on a much higher and elevated frequency. Looking back now, I realise that this was the start of my spiritual journey.

This sensation was one that I would have throughout my life and only now, by using this energy when I work as a medium or healer (a medium is another word for a channel for the spirit world), does it help to balance me. Of course, at that tender age I had no idea that I would eventually develop as a medium. Many of us 'see' or become 'aware' of spirit at a very early age, especially during the first seven years of life, as we have only recently left the world of spirit to be born onto the earth plane and are still relatively close to spirit's vibration. Many of us will remember playing with spirit children but when parents are told, this will often be dismissed and as life goes on our psychic ability usually diminishes. A lot of mediums see spirit relatives when they are very young and this will often be the beginning of their introduction to the world of spirit. We are all psychic, in fact we are 'spirit in a body'. We all have psychic ability but most of us will never use it or indeed develop it, and as we live our earthly lives the majority of us will overlook this other part of ourselves. We are mind, body and spirit and when we come to this realisation, it helps to make us whole.

Also at the age of eleven, I joined the Ivy Travers Stage School in Hackney, East London, where I attended a ballet class every Saturday morning and took part in variety shows that were put on for charity. I was paired up with another girl dancer and I was cast as the boy in a pas de deux (a dance of two), and was given some solo ballet work, this time as a girl! Sadly, the girl pupil that I was partnered with had leukaemia.

Some time ago I was in the audience watching the well-known TV medium, Tony Stockwell, when he linked with me and gave me a message from her. It was lovely to hear from her and obviously she wanted to communicate with me, as you cannot bring spirit through to you if they do not wish to, as they have free will in spirit, exactly the same as we have on the earth plane. It is always love that brings spirit close to us, 'because love overcomes everything', which is something I always say. Of course, when we think about those in the spirit world, it brings them near to us as they pick up our thoughts, as thoughts are living things and go out onto the vibration that is received in spirit, rather like a radio wave or transmitter. I believe that this is how we communicate in spirit, as we only have to think, there is no need to speak, so be careful about what you think!

Through the long road of life
keep your eyes towards Heaven
– Taken from the book 'Wisdom Teachings'.

CHAPTER TWO

My Career in Ballet

I loved ballet and knew that I wanted to dance and it was suggested that I find a school dedicated to ballet training. My mother discovered that there was a hall used for ballet lessons opposite to where we were living at the time in Dalston, East London. By the age of thirteen, I joined Patricia Spalding's School of Russian Style Ballet (known as The Society of Russian Style Ballet Schools).

Miss Spalding, affectionately known to those close to her as Miss S, had had a career in ballet and been a leading lady at The Royal Opera House, Covent Garden, where she had been partnered by the well-known dancer, Anton Dolin. I attended two ballet classes per week until the age of fifteen, when it was decided to leave school to train as a full-time ballet student, with the aim of becoming a professional dancer. Although I started my training at a much later age than most, Miss S told my mother that she felt I was well worth training. Also, at the time Miss S continued with my general education by meeting me at various art galleries and museums in the West End. This also included seeing as many ballets as possible.

Miss S started a private ballet class for me, which I attended for a year, before being joined by two other female students. At the time, I was attending two to three ballet classes per day, which were held from Monday to Friday at a hall in Paddington Street, near Baker Street, West London and on a Saturday at the hall in Dalston. Further dance training included Martha Graham modern, Spanish, character, historical and pas de deux classes, dance notation and working with choreography. I also attended music classes to help me with my musicality and assisted Miss S demonstrating the exercises for the children's classes.

All through these studies, I continued to have out-of-body experiences, a feeling of floating off and being somewhere else, in a type of dream-like state. I would always speak to my father about this, as he had been spiritually aware himself from a young man, and his uncle, who had also been aware of the spirit world for many years, used to talk to my father about spirit.

Later in life, my father became a wonderful healer, as he always worked with love. I remember him telling me that on one occasion he was sending someone deep healing at 8pm one evening and the following day a relative (who was also developing spiritually), telephoned him and asked, 'Did you send healing last night to (and he mentioned the gentleman's name) at 8pm?' My father replied, 'Yes, I did, how did you know?' 'Because,' he said, 'I was with him and I saw you manifest at the side of his bed at 8pm.'

My father was able to guide me with excellent spiritual advice or 'impressions' as he liked to call them. I later learnt that my father was a 'spiritual channel' and whereas others couldn't understand what was happening to me, my father always could. He would be able to balance me and help me to see the lighter side of things, as he had such a brilliant sense of humour.

A very talented young male dancer, who had been a student of Miss Spalding's from an early age, also joined our class and as we were of similar physiques we were paired together for the Annual Schools' Performance, which would follow each year's ballet exams. The male dancer was invited to go to Russia to study further with the Kirov Ballet Company. I was also given the same opportunity to go to Russia but this sent me into a state of panic, due to the constant out-of-body feelings I had been having. I developed a type of agoraphobia since my first experience in Cornwall, and always needed a familiar sound base to be in, which was at home. The thought of travelling so far away filled me with fear, so sadly I never went to Russia to further my career. Later, the male dancer returned and danced with the Royal Ballet, all the richer for his experience.

Meanwhile, I studied ballet intently. My dear mother paid for all of my tuition fees, including ballet shoes, leotards, tights and any other dance requirements I may have needed. At the time my mother was working as a secretary for four partners at a firm of architects in Chancery Lane. After a year of studies, I managed to obtain a series of part-time jobs in the West End, which helped a little financially. One of which was working for the Italian ballet shoe makers, Gandolfi, in the

Marylebone Road, which was a great help as I used to buy my soft and pointe work shoes from them and was also able to try on all of the latest dance wear in my break! During this time, I took all of my ballet exams and also a Teacher's exam, which allowed me to teach children up to the age of eleven.

Looking back, I realise how important both Miss S and my ballet training was for me, as it proved to be a very good grounding in discipline and dedication, both of which I never had before. Miss S was a task master and you would have had to have a good excuse not to attend class. I recall on one winter's evening, Miss S had made the effort to travel from her home in Bayswater to the dance hall in Dalston to take class in fog that was so bad you could hardly see a hand in front of your face. I however, didn't think there would be a class, so I never bothered to go, as just getting across the road could prove dangerous. We then heard a knock at the front door, only to see Miss S standing there and asking me why I wasn't at class and making her intention very clear to me that I should be there! I then hastily got myself over to the hall – and quite rightly so! Again, Miss S expected this type of dedication from all of her pupils. I even took a ballet exam whilst I had scarlet fever, because if you were going to become a professional dancer you would be expected to work through anything and everything. I also recall Miss S telling me that she had to dance on stage the day that her father had passed to spirit. I believe that the earth plane is a school of learning and if you take the tests you learn different lessons, through many lives and that we come back with certain weaknesses and strengths. I now hope that I have added discipline and dedication to my spiritual work.

Just after finishing my dance training, I was fortunate enough to obtain two professional engagements, the first one was for Principal Dancer as the fairy in the pantomime *Babes in the Wood* at the Golders Green Theatre, London. The second engagement was as one of the dancers in the BBC's production of Gilbert and Sullivan's *Iolanthe.* I then took part in the story of *Al Bowlly,* in which I danced the Charleston! I also took part in a show at The Victoria Palace Theatre, London, which saw me dancing with a group of other dancers in a 'Tiller Girl' routine. That takes me back!

Other dance work followed, including Ken Russell's film about the life of Tchaikovsky, called *The Music Lovers*. I then registered with a few theatrical agencies to do some walk-on and extra work, which all helped to make me become a full member of 'Equity', (the 'Actors' Union) and used the stage name of Pauline Dubarry. I was then offered work as a stand in for Penelope Keith in Noel Coward's *Private Lives*, again for BBC television, which was part studio and part location. The location part meant going to Le Touquet, in France, for three days. Until then, I had never been abroad before, as my earlier out-of-body experiences left me with feelings of panic whenever I had to travel, even local trips would leave me with the same dilemma, as mentioned before, as I always needed a familiar and secure base to return to. Anyway, I was committed to the contract and somehow endured it. I now realise that the only way to overcome fear is to face it and work through it, as otherwise you could just trap yourself in a corner and not come out, although it was very difficult to do at the time.

In between work engagements, I used to do some temporary office work, having been fortunate enough to have been taught to touch type by my mother. This was one of the many skills that I had learnt from her and, as my mother used to say, 'I was always able to earn an honest bob!' Another job saw me working behind the bar at the RAF Club in Piccadilly, which allowed me to pay for my first car, a trusty second hand Morris 1000 in Trafalgar blue. I remember going with my parents to choose it and then afterwards feeling very pleased to be able to give my mother a lift to work.

Around this time, I was asked if I would like to do some modelling for a well-known lady artist, to which I agreed. I went to her art studio, in Hampstead for several weeks, where she was able to produce five oil paintings of me. One of these was a portrait and the other four were of ballet poses, in which I wore ballet dresses. Later on, having sold the four ballet paintings, the artist contacted my mother to ask us if we would like the portrait that she had painted of me. My mother said, 'Yes, very much so!' and she sold the painting to my mother for 40 guineas. At the time, it was quite a lot of money, so my mother paid this in two instalments and it happily hung on the wall at home, which I still have to this day.

Through all of this time, I attended ballet classes at the Dance Centre, Covent Garden and would buy *The Stage* newspaper every week, to see what dance work was available. I saw that there was an audition for The London Festival Ballet, to be held at the Sadler's Wells Theatre. I went along to this and whilst dancing I injured the cartilage in my knee, which unfortunately brought the audition to an abrupt end. This to me at the time was devastating and it took eighteen months and a lot of osteopathy before my knee strengthened enough to get back to class; eighteen months is a long time in the life of a dancer. I continued after this for a while with some agency work and it was there that I met my first husband, where we were both extras on the TV programme, *The Suffragettes*. I later married him and we had one daughter, after which my ballet career ended.

If we never stretch ourselves, we never expand
– Taken from the book 'Wisdom Teachings'.

A photo of Pauline which appeared in the magazine *Dance & Dancers*.

CHAPTER THREE

Cat Rescue

Whilst living at home with my parents in North London, I sometimes used to take my mother shopping to Ridley Road Street Market in Dalston, and noticed under a stall a sick black and white kitten. The market men tried to get her but had failed and told me that she was wild (feral). Not to be deterred, I grabbed her and she bit me but I managed to hang onto her, put her in a basket and took her to the local vets, where she was diagnosed with cat flu, which she was then treated for. My then fiancée kept her and called her Lucky!

This was the start of forty plus years of continuous voluntary cat and kitten rescue work. Both my parents, myself and later my daughter, would become involved with helping stray and feral cats and clearing sites due for demolition all around the East and North London areas. Either my father or myself, would drive my mother every evening to feed the cats – my mother always said, 'Everything has a mouth and they all need to eat.' My mother was so dedicated to the cats, they were even fed on my wedding day! Eventually, through perseverance and patience, we cleared the sites. We would trap the cats and transport them to the vets, for either spaying or neutering and to give them any other veterinary help that was necessary. We would then try to find different sanctuaries that would accommodate them, as the sites were going to first be demolished and then re-developed. We would often go out late at night trapping and must have had a lot of protection, as thankfully we never came to any harm.

We also became involved with a small amount of dog rescue and would transport any strays to sanctuaries as well. We used to take cats for treatment to the local RSPCA hospital in Holloway and several of the local PDSA Centres as well. I used to leave my telephone number to help any cats or kittens that couldn't be found homes and otherwise may have been put to sleep. One afternoon, just as I was leaving the hospital with a tabby mother cat and her four kittens, I saw a veterinary nurse rush through to the surgery with two baby kittens, around three weeks old. One was a tabby female and the other was a ginger male. They had just been brought to the hospital, having been found in a garden suffering from cat flu and they were going to be put to sleep as there was very little chance of their survival. I asked the nurse if she would let me take them home and do what I could for them. She agreed but first had to give me a lesson in hand rearing. The nurse then put some flea powder on them and gave me some liquid antibiotics and a dropper.

Sadly, during my journey back the little tabby female kitten passed away, but the little ginger male kitten remained alive. On arriving home, I mixed up his liquid food and had to feed him every two hours and gave him his medication. I found him a warm place in the airing cupboard, to keep up his body temperature and a soft toy to keep him company. The next day I took him to my local vet and after examination the vet said that he didn't hold out too much hope for him (as hand rearing can be tricky at the best of times, together with the added complication of cat flu), and he would be very lucky to pull through – but he did. We kept him and called him Marmalade.

I have always had such a strong belief in the sanctity of all life and I would like to think that over the years, all of the cats and kittens that have been saved have allowed me to add to my healing gift, as I believe that we have to earn everything and nothing is just given to us. Any gifts that we may have, have to be worked at, or otherwise we would lose them.

I remember being in my early twenties when I made the conscious decision to become a vegetarian. It was on Christmas Day, when I saw the turkey on the table being carved and I decided that I no longer wanted to be part of eating anything that had been living.

When we lived in our first house in Seven Kings, Essex, I had four pens put in the garden shed, so that I was able to take strays in myself. I also made contact with other cat ladies in the area and we were usually able to help each other out. A very good friend who runs an animal sanctuary near Colchester, in Essex, used to take the feral cats I had rescued, after spaying or neutering them beforehand. They were then able to live out their lives in a safer environment in the country.

Take care of all living things
– Taken from the book 'Wisdom Teachings'.

CHAPTER FOUR

Healing & Reflexology

When my daughter was aged about two and before I became a healer myself, I heard that Miss S was very ill with cancer and went to visit her at her flat in Bayswater, West London. I suggested that a healer might be able to help her, but she declined as she was an atheist and had no belief in healing or the afterlife and wouldn't change her views. Sadly, not long after this, Miss S passed to spirit. My dear teacher, although without belief, was one of the strongest people I had ever met and had taught me so much by her sheer strength of character and dedication.

For some time, I had a strong feeling that I wanted to try and work as a healer but never knew quite how to go about it. Then the thought came to me that if I studied massage I could help channel healing through my hands. I must have been inspired! I made some enquiries and found a massage course in the West End, which included learning anatomy and physiology. After a while, I acquired my International Therapy Examination Council Certificate (ITEC), and I later added aromatherapy, which uses essential oils to bring about a therapeutic effect. Whilst on the massage course, I met an osteopath and I later assisted him at his practice in Wimbledon, South West London, which was further learning for me.

I was then drawn to reflexology, which is a form of acupuncture, working mainly on the soles of the feet but without using needles. This was practiced in China some 5,000 years ago but updated in America in the 1930s, by a therapist named Eunice Ingham. Without my knowing it at the time, I had a Chinese guide working with me and when you look back everything is part of a pattern or jigsaw puzzle, hence the Chinese connection. This may explain why at the time I was drawn to buying blue and white Chinese pots, ginger jars and temple vases! I was fortunate enough to find a good reflexology teacher, who was also a homoeopathic doctor and I studied with her for about two years and when I had reached a certain standard, she would let me work on her patients to gain experience. In due course, I passed my exam and then started my own reflexology practice, working from home. I never advertised and began with just one patient and then my work gradually increased by recommendation.

During this period of time, I started receiving sayings through my mind (spirit work through the mind), this is known as Mental Mediumship – no laughter please! These sayings were very uplifting and encouraging to me and eventually I was receiving so many messages of a philosophical nature, that I was compelled to write them down, first of all on pieces of paper and then on a note pad. I remember distinctly that on one Good Friday I typed them up using an old typewriter. I had around 2,000 sayings. Later, I was told by my spirit guide, that one day they would be published – and indeed they were! I asked my guide what he wanted the book to be called and he told me – *Wisdom Teachings*. Initially, they were there to help me but eventually they would need to be shared to help guide and uplift anyone who read them. It was during this time that I was going through a difficult period in my life, as my then husband did not share my enthusiasm for either cat rescue work, or indeed my awakening awareness of the spirit world, which of course I understand is not for everyone.

Just after this, I started training at The National Federation of Spiritual Healers, (NFSH), now known as The Healing Trust and in due course passed the assessment held in front of a panel of adjudicators and became a registered spiritual healer. At last, I could use my hands to channel healing (known as touch healing), which seemed to bring about some good results, especially when used in conjunction with my reflexology treatments. I became a registered healer with the NFSH in the year 1991.

I would always offer additional healing after the treatment, should anyone wish and sometimes just giving auric healing (working with the energy field around the body) and helping to balance the seven chakras or energy centres that run through the centre of the body and spread out into the auric field. This is the electromagnetic field that surrounds the body and is shaped like an egg. Also, the auric colours change, depending upon our mood and emotions and I believe that if we stay in a negative mood for a period of time, this could affect the health of the physical body. The aura also has the ability to expand and contract and, for instance, if we find ourselves in a situation where we need to protect ourselves, the auric energy would contract and stay close to our physical body. On the other hand, if we are feeling safe and secure or happy and relaxed, the aura can expand and as I understand it, extend some distance out from the body.

Mostly the hands become very hot, as the healing energy builds up but on rare occasions a cooler energy can be channelled, especially for inflamed conditions. Often healers will send out their healing thoughts and this is known as distant healing or absent healing. Some healers also work with colour healing, this is when a certain colour or colours can be used, channelling the colours through the mind and hands, to bring about a possibly stronger healing effect. For instance, blue is known as a universal healing colour, often used by healers, especially when a cooling and calming colour is required, whereas the colour red can be used when warmth and energy are needed.

While still on the subject of colours, all of the colours in the spectrum have different densities, or vibrations to them. For instance, red is a far denser and earthed colour, together with orange, whereas, blue, indigo or violet vibrate on higher frequencies and tend to be part of our higher selves. Green is a wonderfully balancing colour, (as it is the colour of harmony and nature) and pink is the colour of universal love. Yellow has a very optimistic and positive vibration and golden yellow to white light lifts us towards the spiritual and angelic realms.

Crystal healing can also be used, which harnesses the additional healing qualities found in the crystals and can be held in the hand, or placed on different areas of the body to add further to the healing energies. Another well-known healing method is that of Japanese Reiki and uses powerful symbols to channel the healing energies. I am sure that all of these different forms of healing work well, especially when only the highest healing intent from those giving healing is used.

I went on to run my own reflexology and aromatherapy practice for about twenty-three years, often giving complimentary sessions to those in need.

When you give healing
do it with unconditional love
– Taken from the book 'Wisdom Teachings'

CHAPTER FIVE

The Beginning of My Spiritual Development

The Reading

A round this time, my aunt was sitting in a Development Circle (a place where you attend to develop psychic, mediumistic, trance, healing or any other gifts that you may have). Firstly, I went along to have a reading with the medium, who was about to start a new Development Circle and was a well-known medium from the School of Psychic Studies in London. I remember that I had a very good reading with her and my grandmother, my mother's mother, came through and gave me both evidence and guidance, which I very much needed at the time. I then showed the medium the sayings that I had received and she told me that they weren't from me but from my guide in spirit and I replied that I didn't think they were from me and somehow felt they were coming from some other source, which then confirmed my own feelings about this. The medium then invited me to join her 'Beginner's Circle'.

After my reading, it was as if everything made sense to me and had come into focus, as I could see things more clearly. It gave me a wonderful feeling of wholeness and inner peace. Shortly after this, I joined the medium's circle and it quite literally changed my life.

The Circle

I attended the medium's circle, which was held once a week on a Monday at her home in Ilford, Essex. I felt both nervous and excited about developing spiritually and it was lovely to be taught properly. We originally started with ten people and after about six months of sitting in the circle, the medium told us that out of the ten of us, there were potentially two healers in the group, one of which was a gentleman and the other was myself. In a Development Circle you will often receive confirmation of what you have been given yourself, so that you know it just isn't in your own mind, as we can often influence our own thoughts. It is said that if you receive the same message from three different mediums, there has to be something in it! Sitting in a circle often exposes our own individual strengths and weaknesses and of course you need dedication to attend every week. Unless you have a very good reason for not being there, you should always do so, as the guides make the commitment to be there to work with you, as you develop to become their instrument or channel. A circle quite literally means sitting in a circle, as a circle represents protection and should never be broken. You should always make sure that you sit in the same seat, as your guides become used to your position within the group.

Often, the developing medium can work quite well in a circle, as there is usually someone in it who is like a battery or a power house, adding extra power and energy with which to work with spirit. Each week we were given assorted exercises, with which to work on. One of which was known as psychometry, where you would hold a piece of jewellery, or something similar (only used by the person whose item you would be reading from), as these articles hold vibrations that remain on the jewellery that help you to pick up past events and happenings. We were always told by the teacher, to use the three H's, which represents home, health and happiness, to use as a guideline, if ever we forgot. For instance, 'Did they live in a house or a flat?', 'Did they have any health problems?', or 'Were they happy as a child?' and so on, naturally not asking the sitter any questions but helping us to remember.

Then there were psychic readings, where you would tune in to the person's aura, or energy field and read around them and try to pick up things that had happened in the past and up to the present. Another exercise we used to do was flower clairsentience, a type of sensing, where each group member would pick a flower and bring it along to class and then the flowers were read; this usually started from birth and up to the present time. These types of exercises would be used to strengthen the psychic areas only. The teacher was quite strict with us and would emphasise again and again that when you were giving a reading to someone, you should never ask a question, as it is the medium's job to give what they were receiving directly from their spirit guides. Also, she would emphasise the difference between working psychically and with mediumship.

At other times, we would work with clairvoyance or clear seeing, where we would hopefully start making our connections with the spirit world. Clairvoyance works on developing the 'psychic eye' or the pineal area in the brain, which sits in the forehead and is centred mid-brow. This often starts by seeing symbols, or sometimes pictures and can take a long time to develop. We would tune into spirit by lifting our mental thoughts, or vibrations to an altered higher wavelength, rather like tuning into a radio channel, which can't be seen but can often be felt. Regular meditation helps to tune us into this higher frequency. Most of us will not be aware of the spirit world until we raise our own consciousness and awareness.

Sometimes, we would have a meditation, which enabled us to link around each person in the class, to see what we could pick up, and to give off whatever we received for them afterwards. We were told that no matter how strange or insignificant it seemed to us, we were to give it off anyway and it was usually accurate and meaningful to the recipient. As I developed, I eventually joined the advanced group, of which my aunt was a member. After about two years of sitting in the circle, we were told that we would be trying guide work. Other names used for this are transfiguration, overshadowing, or trance work. This is where you allow yourself to become entranced (in a trance like state), and your guide draws very close, into your energy field or aura. After a lot of developing and dedication, your guide will adjust to your energy vibration and be able to blend and connect with you. A low light and complete silence is required for this type of work, as a bright light or sudden noise could shock you and bring you back into your body too quickly, which could prove harmful, as the spirit world live on a much faster vibration, or frequency, than that of the earth plane. Of course, as you enter into a trance like state you have altered your own vibrational rate to blend more closely to that of your guide's. As you eventually let go and trust your guide, other members of the group can see your facial features change; this is known as transfiguration. This type of work is rare and takes years to perfect and not many people become trance mediums but those that attain this type of work can also bring spirit loved ones through, as loved ones features can manifest on the trance medium's face.

After a time of sitting in the circle, my guide was able to speak through my vocal chords. It takes a lot of trust to be able to stand back and allow your guide to come through. Later, when the teacher gently called me back, I felt a wonderful sense of inner peace and freedom and working with the spiritual energy seemed to ground me, making me feel more rooted and earthed and also eased my constant feelings of anxiety.

Another time, the medium asked us to find out what our guides' names were. I was given the name of my guide, which was Moo Chow Ching, who I was told had lived on the earth plane around 300 years ago and had been a Chinese philosopher. The medium confirmed to me that I did indeed have the correct name – a breakthrough moment, as it then made sense to me why I had been drawn to reflexology and had received all of the philosophical sayings. Guides are very alike to their chosen instruments on the earth plane, hence the blending of personalities but of course they are on a far higher level than us. Our guides quite literally guide us from the spirit world and have infinite patience with us, as they can be developing a potential medium from the beginning of their journey. As mediums develop, other guides can come in and work with them and often the medium (or channel) will soon become aware of these changes. At first, this can make them feel a little uneasy, as they have to adjust to the different vibrations of their new guides. Some mediums work in blind faith and trust, never truly knowing who their guides are and others seem to have several guides, all of which are adding their own individual qualities to the work of the medium.

I once asked my guide a very deep question, to which there was no reply. About two hours later, he came back to me with the answer and I later learnt that he went to ask his guide for the information, who was at a higher level in spirit – I then discovered that even guides have guides!

I sat in the circle for five and a half years and throughout that time managed to do a lot of groundwork, which gave me the foundation to develop and build upon and it also gave me more confidence in becoming a channel for spirit. If you are looking to develop, always look for a circle with a good teacher, who is in control and one who you have confidence in. You should always feel comfortable with those you share the circle with and if you don't and if you seek it, another circle should be presented to you. Over the years, we have also run development circles from our own home. We have always run 'closed circles', which is where the same group of people sit to develop, usually weekly.

Over time, this builds a lot of harmony and trust with which to work. An 'open circle' is more flexible and allows different people to attend as, and when they can, to see if they wish to develop further.

During the time I was sitting in the circle, I had been separated from my husband for several years, as we had grown apart and he sadly did not share my beliefs. I became drawn to the other healer in the group, named Terry, and felt a strong connection with him and my guide kept repeating to me that we would be together one day. Unknowingly, at the same time, Terry had also been drawn to me and consequently made a booking for three reflexology treatments. Since then, Terry has told me that he went through a lot of pain and suffering during the treatment in order to find out more about me! Mind you, he did have sensitive feet!

Being quite shy at the time, I apparently gave him no indication that I was interested in him, so he shelved the idea of asking me out. A few weeks later, a member of the teacher's advanced group was in our circle and said to our teacher, 'I have been told by my guide that I have to give a personal message to Pauline and it has to be given in open circle.' The teacher answered, 'If that's what you've been given, then you had better do it.' The advanced circle member then turned to me and said, 'I am being told that there is a man for you who has been to you for reflexology. He is slightly older than you and has children that are off hand and he is the one for you.' What a message to receive! I then immediately realised that she was talking about Terry and Terry in turn realised that she was talking about him!

One day, shortly after this and while still in the circle, Terry asked me if I would like to meet up with him one evening. In due course, we went out to his local pub for a drink and the conversation flowed and so did the gin and tonics! At the end of the evening, I joined Terry in taking his one-eyed rescue dog, named Nelson, for a walk and in true romantic fashion on a bridge over a river and in the moonlight, Terry took the plunge and gave me a kiss. I then told him, 'I have been waiting a long time for this,' and there and then he proposed to me and I said, 'Yes!' I felt truly at home and we both knew that we had met our soulmates... And so our journey together began – with the help of spirit that is!

When all hearts have the same aim
– things are soon achieved
– Taken from the book 'Wisdom Teachings'

Chapter Six

Moving On

As my life moved on, Terry and I married and over the past thirty years we have shared the spiritual pathway together. As I moved on to helping people with reflexology and healing, my husband's work as a Metropolitan Police Officer came to an end and Terry took on the hands on rescue work with the cats, trapping on sites, in gardens and alleyways and wherever the need arose, also helping other catteries and organisations, including the RSPCA and the Cats Protection League (CPL). All of our rescues are funded by my clairvoyant work, which includes paying the vet bills and any other expenses that occur in helping the cats. My husband continues his work as a healer, using his gift for both people and animals, wherever there is a need and drives me to all of the venues and shares the platform with me when an address (an inspirational talk) is required. Also, whenever I take an evening of clairvoyance for charity, my husband is very good as the Master of Ceremonies. This ability may have stemmed from having to stand up in the dock at The Old Bailey to give evidence!

My First Steps onto the Platform

When we first met, my husband used to give healing at a church in Debden, Essex. It was held on a Friday evening after the church service had finished and was run by a lovely gentleman named Bob Kirk, who was assisted by another gentleman, Reg Golding. I also attended the church to give healing and often Terry and I would give joint healing (combining our healing energies to give an extra boost of healing for those in most need). One evening I was asked by Reg Golding, who himself was a well-known and wonderful medium, to give him some healing. I received a message through for him from spirit and gave this off after the healing had finished. Strictly speaking, you shouldn't combine healing with mediumship but I did so on this occasion. Reg then said he would like me to stand up on the platform with him the next time he was booked at the church, together with another lady who was also a developing medium. I nervously said yes and so it was that the other lady and myself took our first tentative steps onto the platform, in front of an audience, kindly supported by Reg. This is known as a Fledgling Evening, where developing mediums can expand their experience by working in front of people to help them overcome their nerves – although in my experience, it doesn't get much easier! I had felt anxious all week about this but somehow when the day came, I managed to get through it.

Dear Reg Golding was the gentleman who helped me take my first steps onto the platform. Reg has helped and encouraged so many on their spiritual pathways and has been a mentor and true friend and we have much to thank him for. Sadly, dear Reg has passed to spirit now. We were very honoured that latterly he would come to guide us in our home circle and when we work spiritually we are aware that he is with us, as he is very much part of the team.

Sometimes all that is needed
is a word of encouragement
– Taken from the book 'Wisdom Teachings'

CHAPTER SEVEN

Spirit Communication

Little by little, as I worked alongside my Chinese philosopher guide, Moo Chow Ching and after developing further in the medium's circle, I found that when people came to see me for a reflexology treatment I was able to give them some spiritual guidance and sometimes mediumship. As they relaxed during their treatment, I often became aware of a presence building up around them. Usually, this was of a loved one in spirit and with their permission, I would give their description and any messages I had received from them. It is always easier to work with spirit, if the person on the earth plane is in a more relaxed state, as any pre-formed barriers that might exist can be broken down more easily. Often unknowingly, when a person goes to a medium for a reading, otherwise known as 'spirit communication', the sitter can sometimes block themselves from spirit and the medium. This can be caused by fear, as often they do not know what to expect, especially if it is their first ever reading, coupled with their emotion and the emotion of their loved ones around them in the world of spirit. This can cause a huge block and it also depends on how long their loved ones have been in spirit and if they had suffered a long illness before passing, as they may need to rest and recover first, before being able to communicate.

However, some loved ones can communicate within twenty four hours of passing to spirit, so this depends very much on the individual. If they have had any prior spiritual knowledge, or awareness of spirit, before passing over to the light, this will be of great benefit.

I find through linking with those in spirit, if you weren't a good communicator whilst you were here on the earth plane, you will be the same in spirit and vice versa, if you were a good communicator the message usually flows. Everything seems to follow a continuity, rather like going from one room to another. For instance, if you passed to the spirit world in a hospital, you could find yourself in a hospital situation in spirit, being looked after by nurses and doctors and with any loved ones that had gone before you, by your side. As I understand it, those people who worked in caring professions, including counsellors and healers whilst on the earth plane, often continue with the same valuable work in the spirit world.

I have received spirit communication from my husband's mother and also his first wife Ann, both of whom had been nurses whilst on the earth plane. They have both informed me that they are working together in the Halls of Rest (spirit hospitals). This was later confirmed by another medium, who identified them both as nurses, working in the world of spirit.

Another example of spirit communication occured whilst taking an evening of clairvoyance. I gave a message to a medium who was in the audience from his wife in spirit, who herself had been a medium whilst on the earth plane. In conversation with him later, he told me that his wife's role in the 'world of spirit', was to meet and greet people as they passed over to the spirit world. He then went on to tell me that he had been in circle, where he had been receiving communication from his wife, when suddenly she said, 'Sorry, I've got to go now – a ship's just gone down.' When he checked the papers the following morning, he found that a ship had sunk abroad at that precise time, which was confirmation of his wife's work in spirit. I find that whenever I have given a reading to another medium it usually flows, as of course they are far more open and receptive to spirit communication. However, it is more difficult to give off to someone who is emotionally close to us, as we can often influence and colour the answers to a more positive outcome, as it is harder to remain objective.

There will also be a time of reflection and wonderful reunions with friends and loved ones, including their pet animals, which I usually see when working as a channel. I often see a pet bird, or sometimes more than one, flying in from the spirit world and land on the sitter's shoulder and will be shown the colour and breed of the birds also.

When working as a medium, I am often taken into the spirit person's home and shown some of their furniture or favourite ornaments that they used to have when they were on the earth plane. As the energy builds, I feel I can almost reach out and touch the objects in spirit, as they seem so real to me. I feel, if they so wish, they can reproduce the same familiar homes and gardens in the spirit world. I have heard many people describe the beautiful gardens in spirit and how vibrant the colours and smells of the flowers are, and where you can also meet up with up with your friends and loved ones again. I also understand that you can attend concerts in spirit where wonderful celestial music is played.

Every medium works differently, which is, of course, how it should be, as they are each unique in the way that they connect with the spirit world. Most mediums will start their spirit communication by explaining exactly how they work and connect with spirit. Each time a medium links with the spirit world, via their guides, they have no idea who they will be linking with, as each reading is individual and the medium has no script from which to work from. This requires a certain amount of bravery and a great amount of trust, not only in themselves but trust in their connection to the spirit world. Some mediums are very good with names and others have a natural humour with them as they work, as this can often lighten the mood a little, especially if a very deep and emotional link had recently been worked on. I have found that the spirit world like some laughter and if the person in spirit had a sense of humour, they will bring this in with them, as of course they are still the same in character as they were when they lived on the earth plane. In my experience, through working with spirit, I have found that you don't suddenly change, as change takes time and your personality is the same in spirit as it was when you were on the earth plane. I always say that if you want to change – do it now!

Also, if music is played before connecting with the spirit world, it lifts the energy with which to work. It is also important that the person in the audience needs to use their voice when answering the medium (usually by either a 'yes' or 'no'), as when the person in spirit hears their loved one's voice on the earth plane, it helps to connect and strengthen the link with them. If the reply is 'I don't understand', then the medium would normally go back to their guide to bring more information, as it is the medium's job to bring the evidence from spirit, without the need to ask a question from the person they are giving the reading to. I always say that spirit only work through love and the more love that is sent out from the congregation or audience, the more beautiful the link with the spirit world will be.

When I work, spirit will often bring in some spiritual philosophy and guidance, sometimes briefly, as spirit like to educate whenever the opportunity arises. I also see guides around some people and indeed when I am shown either a Nursing Sister, or a Sister of Mercy around someone, I will then realise that the person on the earth plane has given a lot to others and should either have been, or still is, a nurse or a care worker and would be of a compassionate nature. Remember, we always earn everything, including our guides and inspirers. When I see several guides around someone, it is very often the case that this person is a medium and I often identify them as such from the platform.

I also see auric colours around people and some medical conditions, but you should not give medical conditions off from the platform, so as not to worry anyone. When I worked as a reflexologist, I would often inform the patient what condition or conditions they had before they told me! I often see spirit children and when I give this to the person who is receiving the message, this is either a child that they have lost and had lived on the earth plane, or this can represent a miscarriage and the child is living on in spirit. I believe that they don't remain children but continue to grow in spirit. Sometimes, I will receive some privileged information about a forthcoming birth and if the baby will be a girl or a boy, as I either see pink or blue around the baby to let me know what sex they will be.

My guide works with me by giving full details of how the spirit person looked when on earth, usually including the description of the colour of their hair and eyes, and also their character and how they passed to spirit. If lucky, I will be shown the work that they used to do when they were on the earth plane as well. It is very rare though, for me to be given the spirit person's name, as my guide seems to prefer to work with me by giving descriptions, but on some occasions if the spirit person cannot be accepted then my guide will give me their name, which then fully identifies them together with all of the other information I have received.

Another way that spirit can communicate with a person in the audience is that I will see an animal, usually a cat or dog, that would have been either their pet or a spirit person's much loved animal, whilst on the earth plane. I will then follow the progress of the animal, through the audience, until it reaches the person that spirit wish to give a message to. One night, I was taking a clairvoyant evening when I saw a goat in spirit, which led me to a lady and stood beside her. When I described the goat to her, she acknowledged that it had been her pet and because of the love and care she had shown this animal, it wanted to present itself to her again. I am often shown the description of the animal, including their personality and sometimes the pet's passing condition.

I know through seeing so many different animals that they all go over to the light. This can happen if, for instance, someone hand rears a lamb. The animal then becomes more of an individual spirit, rather than a group soul. I believe that when we show any animal unconditional love it will help their progress in the world of spirit.

It is my belief that spirit can project themselves in different ways, either younger or older but usually they present themselves as how they looked when they passed to spirit, for identification purposes. I also believe that when we return to spirit and have had time to adjust, we can go back to a younger age, where we would have functioned at an optimum level, as the spirit world is a very real world and we can then perform whatever tasks we need to do to our best ability. As I have worked as a medium my dear ballet teacher, Miss S (who previously had no belief in spirit), told me that she now learns from me. When I used to give treatments to those with a similar condition to hers, I would often feel her presence draw close to me, as of course she had experienced cancer herself whilst on the earth plane and had empathy with those who were suffering with the same type of illness.

During the years I worked as a reflexologist, I would always link in with spirit whenever the opportunity arose, to give messages to patients and thereby strengthening my connections with the spirit world, as the only way to get better at anything is to work at it!

We can only speak to those who will understand
– Taken from the book 'Wisdom Teachings'

This is a photo of Pauline taking an evening of clairvoyance at the Healing Hearts Spiritual Centre, Bulphan, Essex.

CHAPTER EIGHT

Ann's Story

Ann Lillian Firks – 12.02.42 to 07.02.70

This is the story of my husband Terry's first wife Ann, and how she has communicated through me and others to bring proof of her survival and upliftment to my husband at his time of greatest need.

The story starts over fifty years ago, when Terry was first married to Ann. Ann was a dedicated and caring nurse and her greatest wish was to have children. This proved to be very difficult, as specialists in this field realised it would not be possible without an operation. An operation could not be offered, unless drugs were tried first but they said that in Ann's case, it probably would not work. However, to everyone's surprise Ann became pregnant and gave birth to twin boys, so Ann's greatest wish had been granted.

During this period of time, Ann and Terry were buying their first home together and with a ready-made family, everything seemed to be set fair. However, when the twins were eight months old, Ann said to Terry, 'I want you to listen to me, I know that this is not going to last and I want you to take down my funeral directions.' Ann had never shown any indication that she was mediumistic in any way, but she seemed to know for certain that something was going to happen. Two months later, as a result of a tragic accident, Ann passed to the world of spirit, leaving Terry with twin boys of ten months old.

The following sixteen years proved to be the most difficult and challenging years in Terry's life, until he did a job for an older lady. Afterwards, whilst sitting on the settee and having a cup of tea with her, he noticed the lady was looking at the end of the settee and she said to him, 'Please don't be alarmed, but your wife is sitting on the end of the settee with you and she is keeping an eye on you so that you can keep an eye on the two boys.' It transpired of course that this lady had been a medium and she said to Terry, 'I am retired but your wife obviously wants to talk to you and I can recommend a good medium for you to see'. Terry booked to see the medium a month later. In the meantime, Terry also met a lady who was a member of a medium's circle and in conversation he mentioned that he would be interested in joining a beginner's circle, if ever an opportunity arose. A week later, this lady contacted Terry and said, 'You won't believe this but our medium is starting a beginner's circle and she is now interviewing people and here's her telephone number!' Nothing ever happens by chance. Terry telephoned and made an appointment to see the medium and at the interview Terry stated that he did not see or hear anything in the spiritual sense but was just interested. The medium just smiled and said, 'I will see you on Monday!'

On the Friday before joining the circle, Terry went to see the medium who had been recommended to him. Immediately, the medium said, 'I have your wife, father and dad here, that's your wife, her father and your dad.' During the half hour recorded reading, the medium said, 'Your wife's name is Ann and she was a nurse. Your wife is showing me a chain around your neck,' and Terry immediately said, 'I don't wear any jewellery,' and the medium answered, 'Wait a minute, I am being shown a cross on the end of the chain.' Terry said, 'I was given a cross by my daughter at Christmas and I have just bought a chain but I haven't put them together yet.' The medium said, 'Your wife is telling me that she has been instrumental in you getting this and you are to wear it for your own protection,' and my husband wears the cross to this day. At the end of the reading the medium said, 'I am being told that you are right on the threshold,' and Terry replied, 'Well the only thing new that I am doing is that I am about to join a medium's circle on Monday.' The medium just smiled, stood up and shook his hand and that was the end of the reading.

On the Monday Terry joined the new beginner's circle. I also joined the circle on the same day and this was the first time that I met my future husband. There were ten of us in the circle and one of the other members was called Diane. Diane proved to be very gifted but unfortunately suffered from arthritis and was unable to drive at times, so Terry used to collect her to take her to class. The circle had been running for about a year when Diane went on a week's residential calligraphy course in June of that year. On the first Monday of the course she described not being able to concentrate all day, so in the evening she sat under a tree in the garden and meditated. She said that Ann had come straight through to her and said, 'I have been trying to get though to you all day because I want you to do a poem for my husband, Terry.' Ann gave Diane the first line of the poem and Diane said that she knew the poem and would carry out her wishes. Then Ann said that she wanted it to be delivered on a particular day in August. When Terry collected Diane for class on this day in August, Diane handed him this beautiful framed poem and said, 'Ann has told me that I have got to deliver it to you today – but I don't know why?' Terry just smiled and said, 'It's because it's my birthday.' Terry was on his own at this time and was probably at one of the lowest points in his life, so to receive this was truly uplifting. The words of the poem are:-

Think of me at night when sleep is near
and I who love you am so far away.
Think of me and I will come to you

nor leave you until night turns into day.
Stretch forth your hand and through the depths
of dark
another hand shall touch your fingertips,
and as of old my voice shall breathe your name,
and press a kiss upon your dreaming lips.

A few months later, one of Terry's twins was passing out from college and went up on stage to receive his certificates and diplomas; this was when Terry sent his thoughts up to Ann to say that he hoped that she could see all that was going on and was as proud of their son as he was. This took place at 4pm. At 8pm that evening Terry attended the circle and that night one of the members of the advanced circle was at the meeting and she tapped Terry on the shoulder and said to him, 'I don't know if this makes any sense to you but I have to give you a message from your wife and she says that the thoughts that you sent up to her, as your son walked up onto the stage were received.' Of course, in spirit you can communicate by the power of thought, as all thoughts are heard, so as already mentioned, be careful what you think!

At the time, we both worked as healers at our local spiritualist church and it wasn't long before wedding bells were sounding. On the eve of the wedding Ann came through to me to say that she would be at our wedding to give us her blessing. After the wedding, we went back to our local spiritualist church and took our wedding photographs with us, as a number of people from the church had attended our wedding. My husband had the album open at the first page, showing us together at the entrance of the wedding venue. At that moment, the mediums for that night entered, who were Greater World mediums. They were Pat and Bill Baker, whom we had never met before. Bill Baker looked over my husband's shoulder at the photograph and said, 'What a lovely photograph but do you know who the other lady is standing the other side of you with long black hair and wearing a cape?' My husband said, 'Yes, I do,' and Bill said, 'It was your first wife. Do you know why she was there?' My husband said, 'Yes I do,' and Bill said, 'She was there to give you her blessing,' and my husband said, 'Thank you very much Bill that is confirmation.'

About a year later, I was just going off to sleep one night, when I had a message from my guide in spirit and I turned to my husband and said 'I have a privileged message for you from the world of spirit – I have been told that your first wife, Ann, had been a nun in a previous life and had only come back this time to experience child birth, so when she returned to the world of spirit it did not cause her a problem because she knew she was here for only a short period of time.'

Ann has been a wonderful communicator and I have often seen her (through my psychic eye), in her navy cape, with red lining and her lovely long black hair. Ann would often communicate with me when grandchildren were due and also as to what sex they would be, often before his own children knew! As mentioned earlier, I have had information through that Ann is continuing her work as a nurse in the Halls of Rest in spirit. When my husband's mother, who had also been a nurse, passed to the world of spirit, she informed me that she has joined Ann, where they continue to work as nurses, on the other side.

In 2015, my husband had a sudden collapse with sepsis and at one time was only given two to three hours to live. Fortunately, he survived to tell the tale! A year later, I was taking a clairvoyant evening in Hertfordshire and the lady who was chairing for me and who I had never met before, gave me a wonderfully evidential message for Terry, and said, 'When your husband was seriously ill and close to passing, there were two nurses by his side and they never left him, one was his mother and the other was a lady called Ann.' What a fantastic message to receive, which proves beyond doubt that those we truly love, never leave us and draw close to us during times of great need.

My husband asked me, out of interest, 'How do loved ones in the world of spirit know when we are close to passing?' I said, 'I will ask my guide,' and he replied, 'From the world of spirit we appear as a light and when our light starts to dim, our loved ones know that we are close to passing and draw near to help us over to the spirit world.'

What is created in love cannot be destroyed
– Taken from the book 'Wisdom Teachings'

CHAPTER NINE

Spiritual Guidance – But in a Different Way!

Some time ago, we decided to visit John o' Groats in Scotland, as we had visited Land's End the year before and thought it would be nice to visit the opposite end of the country as well. Have car – will travel! We had to take the trip during the school holidays, as my daughter was then still in primary school. We hadn't booked anywhere in advance to stay and were just trusting to luck!

On the first day we managed to travel to Inverness, in the Highlands. We saw a vacancy sign outside a guest house, so we booked in and the landlady said, 'You're lucky, as I've only just put the sign out.' When she realised that we hadn't made any prior bookings, she warned us that everywhere was fully booked in Scotland due to it being the school holidays. Despite the landlady's warnings, the following day we made our way to John o' Groats. After spending a lovely day there, we decided to make for Ullapool, a well-known tourist destination. As we started driving there, my husband looked at his watch and said, 'We won't get to Ullapool until about 8pm tonight and we're not likely to find a place to stay.' With that, I spoke to my guide, Moo Chow Ching and he informed me that this wouldn't be a problem as they had already reserved a place for us! I told my husband this and he raised an eyebrow but didn't question it! On arrival in Ullapool, about 8pm, we joined a queue of cars driving around the town, looking for a place to stay. We tried one place, without success and then we saw another guest house with a sign outside. My husband went and knocked on the door and the landlady told my husband that the room was already taken but that she had left the sign outside so that the people could find it more easily. At the same time that my husband was talking to the landlady I saw my guide sitting on the roof of the guest house! He told me that we would be staying there tonight!

When my husband returned to the car, I told him what my guide had said and asked him to go back to speak to the landlady again. He then returned to the guest house and asked her how long was she going to give the people who had booked the room and she said at least another hour. My husband then replied, 'We've only just arrived and we need to get something to eat, so is it alright if we come back in an hour's time?' My husband then said, 'I take it that you have a family room,' and she replied, 'Yes, as a matter of fact I have.' An hour later we returned to the guest house, to see a couple standing on the doorstep but still felt confident that the room was for us! The landlady then dismissed the couple on the doorstep and walked across to our car and said, 'The room is yours!'

As we carried our cases across the road to the guest house, my guide told me that there was a man in the house who smoked a pipe and although this seemed insignificant at the time, I mentioned this to my husband. During the rest of the evening and also at breakfast in the morning, there were no signs of either a man or a pipe! When my husband went to pay the bill, he had to enter the landlady's private living quarters, where he noticed a pipe in the grate. On seeing this, my husband asked, 'Who smoked the pipe?' She replied that it was her husband's and that he was disabled and didn't show himself. Upon which, my husband told her the story of what Moo Chow Ching had said. The landlady looked utterly amazed and told my husband that she couldn't believe how calm we were last night, when we should have been panicking. My husband said, 'We weren't panicking because we knew that the room had already been reserved for us.' I can still remember the look of amazement on the landlady's face as we drove away!

How to Find a Home Without an Estate Agent!

Some years ago, my husband was involved in property renovation and this brought in another guide, who appeared to me as a young Indian prince on an elephant and whose name I understood was Rajah. Whenever a property restoration was due, he would appear to me riding on his elephant, carrying a chest of gold and shortly afterwards another project would present itself.

A lady, who was a medium herself, used to come to me for reflexology treatment and one day as she was lying on my practice couch, she said to me, 'I have an Indian boy here on an elephant, does this make any sense to you?' I said, 'Yes, I know who he is, his name is Rajah and he shows himself to me in the same way.' It is always good when you can receive confirmation from another source.

For some time, we had been looking for another property to move to, as we wanted a quieter and safer location for the cats and us! In fact, we had been looking for about two years. One evening, when we were sitting at home, Rajah appeared to me on his elephant and I saw that he had brought another herd of elephants with him. Rajah then proceeded (through my psychic sight) to load up all our furniture onto the elephants and leave through the front door. I told my husband this and he said, 'Quick, which way is he turning?' I said, 'He's turning left.' My husband then said, 'Follow him!' I then followed Rajah and the other elephants for about ten miles (in my mind of course), until he came to a roundabout, where he stopped. It later transpired that there was a bungalow in need of renovation in the first road, just off of the roundabout, which is where we are living today. Thanks to Rajah and spirit that is!

The above is an example of something which is known as precognition. This is when we are able to receive information from spirit about a future event, such as the forthcoming birth of a child, or a change of residence or career. This is possible because as mentioned before, the spirit world exists on a faster vibration or frequency than that of the earth plane and these events have already occurred in spirit.

Life is a mystery to those who don't understand it!
– Taken from the book 'Wisdom Teachings'

Chapter Ten

Rescue Work

As my gift developed, I used to get asked to give the occasional private reading and I was invited back to Bob Kirk's church twice a year, to work in front of a congregation and take a service. During this period, we also started our own home circle, which gave me the opportunity to work as a teacher and help to develop others. As time went by, I used to do group readings, where I would give a reading to each one in turn, monies from which always went to help the cats. One day, we decided to hold an evening of clairvoyance from home, again to fundraise for the cats and kindly a few other mediums offered their services for free. Sitting in the audience was another medium and it later transpired that she was a rescue medium, which at the time I knew very little about. Later we became friends and she would sometimes come along as a guest to our circle.

Quite soon, after meeting the rescue medium, I was invited to give readings to a group of ladies in Hertfordshire. I read my first few and then while working with one of the ladies, I saw this gentleman in spirit around her, which turned out to be her late husband. I saw him in a wheelchair and he seemed quite anxious and kept moving around the room. All of a sudden it appeared that I was being blocked by this gentleman in spirit but when the lady left the room, her husband accompanied her and then my connections would become clear again. At the time, I was very confused with what was happening. When I next met up with my friend I told her what had happened with the one particular reading and she said that this was a rescue and I should have dealt with it at the time. I explained that this was a new situation to me and that I didn't know how to deal with it, she then proceeded to show me how to do this and involved me with my first rescue. I now realise how important it was for me to have met her, as spirit must have brought her to me that evening and since then I have become involved with rescue work.

During this time, I did countless rescues – let me try to explain how it works. For example, some people after passing will stay at Euston Station, when they really need to be in Scotland, or instead of being on the ground floor of a house, they need to be on the top floor. I am purely used as an instrument on the earth plane to communicate with those in spirit that may need a little help to guide them on their way.

Whenever I was giving a reading and I became aware that a rescue, or a helping hand was needed, I would describe the spirit person and give details of them to the sitter and sense that they were very close to the earth plane and then try to establish why they hadn't moved on. I would then become aware of another spirit loved one, who came in from the light and once the spirit person, who needed a helping hand became aware of their loved one, they would be very happy to go with them over to the light. I have found that if the person who had passed, had sadly been without any loved ones or friends around them and perhaps they may have loved music, I would become aware of this and then the sound of the music would help to draw them over to the light, together with the help of my rescue guides. I have two rescue guides who help me, one is an Irish nun named Sister Bernadette and wears a black and white habit. The second rescue guide is a Salvation Army lady named Sister Mary, who told me that whilst living on earth she rescued souls in need and continues to do the same in spirit.

Also, when spirit stay close to the earth plane, they can sometimes cause material disturbances. For instance, if they want to let their loved ones know that they are around them, they can move objects or cause electrical disturbances, such as switching lights on and off. It is known that the energies of a disturbed teenager can also bring about psychic disturbances. I have also been aware that spirit who are close to the earth plane can draw off a loved one's energy, but after a rescue takes place the loved one on the earth plane can look visibly brighter. Also, physical presence can manifest itself through the smell of flowers, perfume and tobacco smoke, all favourites of the person in spirit to let you know that they are around.

Sometimes, our loved ones in spirit will influence songs or music on the radio, that would have had a special meaning or memory to us. Also, we can sometimes feel when a loved one is near, often sensing them out of the corner of our eye but when we look up their presence has disappeared. This is because they can move very quickly in spirit and would never wish to frighten or alarm us. Our loved ones can come close to us in dreams, as we are usually in a more relaxed state and it makes it easier for them to connect with us. I am sure we can all remember having a vivid dream, where we met with our loved ones and thought that it had really happened, only to wake up and realise it was just a dream. When spirit draw close, they can sometimes bring a sensation, which feels a bit like a cobweb on your face. Another way spirit loved ones can let us know they are with us is that we may actually feel their physical touch.

I would like to point out that when these things happen, this doesn't necessarily mean that the spirit person is in need of rescuing, as spirit can come close to us just because they want to make their presence known. Indeed, if we have been thinking or speaking about our loved ones, or have recently been looking through photos of them, this also brings them close to us as they are only a thought away.

Once at a clairvoyant evening, a lady asked me if I could help with a problem in her house. I said I would see what I could do and half-way through the demonstration spirit took me to the lady (spirit are always the control and you have to work with who they take you to). As I linked with her, I became aware of a gentleman who had previously lived in her house and as I described him the lady understood his description, as she had met him on a prior occasion. I was given that the gentleman used to warm himself by the fireplace in the living room but that it was no longer there and he felt confused by this. The lady then confirmed that they had removed the fireplace and had made other alterations. No wonder the gentleman in spirit was confused, it used to be his home and new people were occupying his space. The poor gentleman had become fearful and muddled and sadly hadn't moved on. I was then aware of a mother figure in the distance and I was able to connect him with his mother and she collected him and took him back to the light. Rescues are often emotional but there is a great sense of lightness and upliftment afterwards. At later dates, when asking about the rescues, confirmation has come back that all has settled and they no longer feel the presence of the spirit person.

I feel it is very important to mention here that when loved ones are helped over to the light, and often after resting and familiarising themselves with their new surroundings, they will fully link back with their loved ones on the earth plane but on a much higher frequency, which will enable a clearer communication in the future. People often feel that they will lose contact with their family or friends when they go to the light but this is not the case at all, it is just that they are where they should be now and there was a slight delay in getting there. May I add here, that time appears to be different in the spirit world (a little faster), so I feel that those who have been around the earth plane will not have felt that they were there for long. As with all things, it is very individual in each case. I would like to mention that all I feel I am doing is giving those in need a helping hand. These are everyday, normal people who have passed to spirit and I am merely used as a helper.

There are also other types of rescue. Indeed there are people who sit in circle with the specific purpose of doing rescue work. Of course, there is power in numbers and often this extra power will be needed, as some rescues can be very difficult and will take a stronger medium or circle to deal with them. So far I have not ventured into this area. Also, there are group rescues that can be done, where many souls can be helped over to the light at the same time. I would also like to say that there are many people or mediums that don't feel that rescue work is necessary and that we all go over to the light straight away, but in my experience I feel that what I and others have done has been of great value.

Looking back, it is interesting to see that I have spent most of my life rescuing! This started with the rescue of cats and then my involvement with spirit rescues. Again, it has followed a pattern or continuity throughout my life so far.

A few years ago, whilst on holiday with my husband on the Isle of Wight, a place known for its spiritual activity, we visited a manor house which was known to have many spirits in it. The manor house dated back to the twelfth century. There were organised tours and as the next one was still a little time ahead, we decided to visit the gardens of the house first. We found a seat and I became aware of many monks from the spirit world around us. I later learnt that the house had been used as a monastery going way back. I asked my guide in my mind if they were alright. My guide replied that they were all in the light but that they had left an impression behind, rather like a video recording.

We later joined a small group of people for the guided tour of the house. The tour guide was a lady dressed in period costume of the time and she proceeded to tell us about the manor's history, room by room. The lady then said that there had been a history of spirit sightings in the house and she would be pleased to hear from anyone, at the end of the tour, who had seen or felt anything whilst walking around. As we toured the property, I became aware of a young spirit girl, around the age of twelve, with long blonde hair and wearing a blue dress. At the end of the tour we waited behind and we had a word with the tour guide. I mentioned to her that I was a medium and described the young girl that I had seen and who was now standing beside her. The lady tour guide was very surprised and said that she had been aware of her for some time and had felt her tug her skirt and touch her hair. The tour guide was herself familiar with spirit, as she was sitting in an awareness group (a type of pre-circle). We were standing in one of the oldest parts of the building, where the monks used to kneel and pray, when I suddenly became aware of my Sister of Mercy and I realised then that spirit wanted to use me to help the young girl over to the light.

I told the tour guide that I was a rescue medium and asked her if it would be alright to help the young girl over to the light. The tour guide said that she would be only too happy if the young girl could be rescued. Then, we all felt the room go icy cold, a sign spirit were close and I knew I was being used by them to help. I spoke to the young girl (mind to mind) and told her that it was her time to leave the house and to go across to the light, and with the help of my rescue guides, I saw her spiritually crossing *a bridge to the light.* After the rescue, we all felt very cold and were pleased to step outside into the warmth of the afternoon sunshine.

I wanted to ask my guide further about what had just happened and then the tour guide joined us and said that there was no one waiting for the next guided tour, something that had never happened before. My husband said that spirit must have organised this so that we could all speak together. The tour guide, knowing the history of the house, told us that she had appeared to other people in the past and then sadly informed us, that this young girl had met an untimely demise, due to her life having been taken. Apparently, this young girl dated back to the seventeenth century, my oldest rescue to date. How wonderful that this had all been organised by spirit. First of all, our visit to the manor house and the fact that the house had remained the same throughout the centuries, and also that the tour guide was wearing the same type of clothes of the period that the young girl was used to. All was so familiar to the young girl that this may have been the reason why she had been so drawn to the tour guide.

Intrigued to find out if the young girl had gone over to the light, we agreed that we would meet up the next day to discuss what had happened. The tour guide confirmed to us that she no longer felt the presence of the young girl. We can only hope that she is now fully at peace. We later learnt that the manor house is no longer open to the public and were really pleased to have helped with this rescue and so was the tour guide.

Yet another example of rescue work took place when I was asked to give a reading to a lady who had sadly lost her father at an early age and, although she had attended many public demonstrations of clairvoyance, no medium had ever linked with her and therefore she had not received any proof of survival from her father. Sometimes, when a person was of a shy nature, they do not always come through to their loved ones in a public demonstration and often prefer to communicate in a private one-to-one reading. This could have explained why the lady had never received any communication from her father. Another reason for lack of communication could be that there was a breakdown of the relationship which could strain matters. Other reasons might be that the person is still resting in spirit and of course those in spirit have to learn how to connect and work though a medium's vibrations, thereby connecting the two worlds together.

During this reading, the first spirit person that came through was the lady's grandmother, her father's mother, who was a good communicator.

As mentioned before, I have found that you have the same personality in spirit as you had when you lived on earth and those with better communication skills are easier to link with, but I have to say that love conquers all. As the reading continued, I became aware of a male spirit sitting in my aura and I had a feeling of a great weakness with him. This has happened to me so many times before, when the spirit person will use my energy, only temporarily, to build up and become stronger and familiarised with their surroundings, as if they were just waking up after a deep sleep. Whilst I am being used as a channel for both mediumship and rescue, I seem to work in a semi-trance like state, allowing myself to be momentarily taken over, which requires all of my concentration.

As I described the gentleman and that he had passed with a cancerous condition, the lady realised I had at last got her father. He then told me that he had a great fear of dying, coupled with the fact he had no knowledge of the spirit world and this was the reason why he never moved on. I was then able to talk to him and say that his dear mother had come to collect him to take him back to spirit for rest and healing, and I asked my two rescue guides for help (although they would do this automatically). I then felt him leave my energy and move across to his mother and she took him over to the light. After this happened, both the lady and myself felt a great sense of relief and upliftment.

I then said to the lady that hopefully in the future, if she attended any further clairvoyant evenings, her father should be able to link with her now that his consciousness has been raised and after he had fully restored and healed in spirit. I later learnt that the gentleman had passed to spirit at the very young age of thirty, and that his daughter felt that part of her life was missing because of losing her father when she herself was so young. After having experienced the communication with her father it set her mind at rest and a major piece of life's jigsaw puzzle had fallen into place for her.

The following year, the same lady requested a further reading with me. From my point of view it would be interesting to see how her father had progressed in spirit and if he was ready to communicate. Straight away he linked in and was full of vitality but seemed a little agitated. Yet again, I felt another spirit presence sit in my energy field but this time it was an older gentleman and as I described him and how he had passed to spirit, the lady recognised him as her grandfather, her father's father. This gentleman had also passed away with the same type of cancer that his son had had. I then realised why his son was there and seemed so agitated, as he was eager to rescue his father, the same way he himself had been rescued the year before. On recognising his son, the father then was happy to leave my aura and go over to the light, via the rescue guides. This in fact turned out to be a double rescue, which I had never experienced before. How wonderful that the lady's father a year later, and through both knowledge and understanding, was then able to help his own father.

Often in a reading, the sitter is only interested in receiving communication from one particular loved one but sometimes other family members or friends will link first, as they may have been in spirit longer and are more used to linking and of course may have been stronger characters. Whilst it can frustrate the person coming for the reading to have to sit through other spirit links, it is often necessary, especially when a rescue is required, as they will be put in place first to help the spirit that needs rescuing, often bringing comfort and strength to them. Being a medium is only a channel and we have no control over who wishes to communicate. I have found though that the name of the person in spirit will usually help to bring them forward, so I ask the sitter if they would give me their loved one's name and once called out it seems to help the spirit person become more focused, as our name is a major part of our personality, who we were and of course who we still are.

Another rescue that stands out for me, is that of a First World War soldier. A lady who had been coming to me for reflexology treatments and also knew that I worked as a medium asked me for some spiritual help and advice. Apparently, when she had bought her 150 year old farmhouse she was told of the spirit presence of a young soldier. She herself had not been aware of him but her two grandchildren, who at the time were both aged under seven (and remember we are very close to spirit at that age), had seen him walking along the upstairs landing. Immediately, projected into my practice room, I saw a young man dressed in the uniform of a First World War soldier, whose head was bandaged and who was carrying a rifle and whom I assumed had died from his injuries. Close behind him I saw a nurse dressed in the style of the period and an old ambulance with a red cross on it. Also, in the distance was an older gentleman, whom my guide told me was the soldier's father. I asked the soldier what had happened to him and he replied that he had shot people during the war. Being of a sensitive nature this had deeply troubled him and through his own guilt had not been able to move on. I then told him that he himself had been shot and I was impressed to tell him that it was time to forgive himself, as he had suffered long enough. I saw that his father was waiting to be reunited with him, and with the assistance of the spirit nurse and the spirit guides, he was helped over to the light.

Another reason for not moving on, is that we can hold ourselves back by guilt and remorse and this young soldier had been caught up in the horrors of war, fighting for his country. As I understand it, we judge ourselves in spirit and this of course can be a very painful experience, as in spirit our sensitivity to everything is infinitely increased. In this rescue, the lady that came for reflexology was the connection that brought attention to this situation, even though she was not related to the young soldier. I found out later that this lady had done some research on the previous owners of the farmhouse and discovered that around a hundred years ago, a farmer lived there and had a son that had been killed in the First World War.

Although rescue mediums are often asked to attend houses or places where spirit have been seen, I have found that by talking about the situation help can be given from anywhere, as was the case in this rescue which took place in my practice room. The guides would have been aware in advance of what was about to take place and in spirit distance is no barrier. Everything that is done with rescue is done in spirit's time and law, as spirit are always the control.

Another interesting rescue took place when a lady came out for a reading. As I opened the door to her I could see a spirit lady so close behind her that she was in the lady's aura, or energy field. When she sat down I asked her if she realised that there was a lady from spirit so near to her and she replied that she had no idea of this. I then went on to describe the lady, her character and how she had passed to the spirit world and she immediately recognised her as a good friend of hers when she was on the earth plane. I then picked up that the sitter was very tired and drained and had been suffering with depression and felt that her friend in spirit had been drawing off or using her energy, which had left her exhausted. I then realised that I would be used to do another rescue.

The sitter was a motherly lady and had been very kind and understanding to many people during her lifetime and that is why the spirit lady had drawn close and didn't want to leave her, because she felt safe around her. As the reading continued, I said to the lady in spirit that it was time for her to leave her friend's energy and go over to the light, as I was aware of the spirit guides drawing near, but the spirit lady seemed very reluctant to leave her friend's energy. I asked her why this was and she replied that as a child she had been abused by her father (who himself was now in spirit), and was frightened that she might meet up with him again. My guide then told me that her father was being held at a lower level in spirit and unless she herself chose to, she would not have to meet up with him again.

As I understand it, in spirit you can visit a lower level but you cannot go to a higher level until you have earned the right to do so. I then told the lady in spirit what my guide had told me and only after this reassurance would she leave her friend and go across to the light. After this rescue took place, the sitter looked visibly brighter and I could see that her aura had cleared. I felt her depression would lift and that her full vitality would be restored.

I believe that everything that we do on earth is taken back with us to spirit, both good and bad and that we earn the level at which we return to as there are many levels in the spirit world. This is why I believe that we live many lives, and as we correct ourselves and balance things out we make advancement, and so we eventually become whole and we do not have to come back to the earth plane again.

Over the years, I have been used as a channel for rescue work whilst engaged in everyday activities. I remember whilst out in Spain helping my mother's charity, the Costa Blanca Feral Cat Trust (CBFCT), my husband and I were trapping some cats to take back to the surgery for sterilisation and whilst putting the cats into the van, I was chatting to the English lady who owned the villa. The lady had always been nervous of spirit but I could see a gentleman from the spirit world building up around her and I felt he was her father and in need of help. I gave off to her what I had seen and quickly, there and then in the street I did a rescue. The lady was quite amazed by what had happened and I remember saying to her that this was multi-tasking! I have done so many rescues whilst on holiday, in restaurants, a bank, a casino on a cruise ship, and even when I was having my hair tinted!

We recently visited a 110 year-old farmhouse in Gloucestershire, where relations were picking up a spirit presence and I was called upon to help. As I walked around the property, I came to a room on the ground floor where I sensed the presence of an elderly lady who used to play the piano. The present owner confirmed that an elderly lady had indeed been the last occupant and also that he had found some piano music in the property. I felt that this was the room that the lady had passed away in and that her spirit was still around. It transpired that the lady had lived there all her life and had never married. With the help of my rescue guides, I was able to help her over to the light. The occupants later confirmed that they no longer felt a spirit presence in the property. We sadly learnt that the lady had passed away some seven years previously but had remained around the earth plane ever since, with possibly not having any prior knowledge or understanding of the spirit world and chose to remain in familiar surroundings.

I do believe that some prior knowledge or awareness of the spirit world will aid our progress when we pass over. For example, my dear father, who had a wealth of spiritual knowledge and understanding, was able to communicate back to me via another medium just 48 hours after he passed. My dear mother communicated with me two weeks after her passing, through a message given to me by a medium at a spiritualist church. Communication from my mother-in-law took three months and so on – so spiritual knowledge does help to aid your progression and acclimatisation on the other side. In a later communication with my father, he described the beautiful colours and smells of the flowers in spirit and that they all grew together, and I later learnt that all of the flowers grow together because there are no seasons in spirit.

It is my belief that if you are open to spirit, you can be used for the greater good. I have learnt to be more adaptable than I ever have been before, as help can be given in any place and at any time, not only when it has been formerly arranged, as of course you may never be in that place or time again – with the blessing of spirit that is.

In helping others we help ourselves
– Taken from the book 'Wisdom Teachings'

Chapter Eleven

The Hall of Mirrors

Some years ago, my husband's mother passed to the world of spirit. Three months after she passed, she came through to me with a message for my husband. She said, 'I have been to the Hall of Mirrors.' I asked her, 'What do you mean?' and she said, 'I have been made to look at myself, I helped a few people while I was here and so they don't think too badly of me, so I am alright.' My husband's mother was quite a character and this is the sort of way that she would have communicated.

A few years later, my husband's daughter decided to try for a third child and in a meditation I was given that if she went for a third child, there would be serious problems. I told my husband about the information I had received and he in turn informed his daughter, but contrary to this advice she went ahead and became pregnant.

When she gave birth she haemorrhaged so badly that she went into cardiac arrest and was rushed into theatre, where she was given twelve units of blood and had to be defibrillated to bring her back.

Sometime later, my husband's daughter, in conversation with her father, said, 'Did I ever tell you what happened to me when I gave birth to my third child?' His daughter then went on to tell him of the near death experience that she had had. During this near death experience she described travelling through the tunnel towards the light, feet first. My husband's daughter then said that she entered into an area in spirit called The Hall of Mirrors and recalled the area as being surrounded 360 degrees by tall mirrors. There was no one else there, just a bright light and she said that she was made to look at her life and realised that everything that she had done in her life, so far, had been recorded.

Eighteen hours later, when she recovered consciousness in the hospital ward, she realised that she had to do something with her life and this is why she trained as a nurse. My husband's daughter obtained a nursing degree and is now an Advanced Nurse Practitioner. He asked her how she knew it was called The Hall of Mirrors, bearing in mind the earlier message that he had received from his mother. She said that as she went through the tunnel towards the light she was told in her mind that she was going to the Hall of Mirrors. Then my husband asked, 'How long did the journey take through the tunnel towards the light?' and she said, 'It felt like about four minutes.' My husband then asked me, 'Why is there a time delay?' I asked my guide and he told me that the earth plane is on a slower vibration and the world of spirit is on a faster vibration, and during your journey through the tunnel towards the light you are speeding up to the faster vibration of the spirit world.

There is a record of everything
– Taken from the book 'Wisdom Teachings'

Chapter Twelve

The Wonder of Animals

Some years ago, I was asked to rescue a tortoiseshell cat in Hackney, East London, who was skin and bones and heavily pregnant and the local children were throwing stones at her. I rushed down with a trap and was able to catch her. When I returned home, I placed her in a pen in our cattery and wondered if she was a friendly domestic cat or a feral, in other words, friendly or not. I then started to talk to her and she came forward and I thought, I don't think she's feral – so I opened up the pen door and she placed a paw on either side of my neck, as if hugging me to say 'Thank you'. I was so delighted that she was now safe. Needless to say, we kept this one and named her Chloe.

Another feral cat, a three-month-old black kitten, which my husband, Terry, had rescued proved very difficult to tame but my husband persisted in cuddling him, whether he wanted it or not! Terry eventually won him round, despite his protest! We decided to keep this one as well and called him Midnight. Unfortunately, just three months later, he was knocked down and killed on the road. This young cat had really got under my husband's skin and he asked me what was all that about, after all the effort he had put in. I asked my guide and the information I was given from spirit was that the cat, who had come to us as a feral, had been advanced spiritually by the love that he was given and so had helped his progression. I believe that the love that we show animals truly helps their souls to advance.

In the past, when my parents went on holiday to Wales, outside the hotel where they were staying, they saw a ginger tomcat, who they noticed had a problem with his mouth and eyes. My parents then asked the hotel owners if he belonged to anyone and if he was being fed. They said, 'No, we don't encourage him in here, he's a stray and just gets a few scraps from our guests.' As the hotel would not let him in and he never had an owner, on my parents return home some Welsh cat rescue organisations were contacted, the nearest one being twenty miles away, and they said that they were unable to help, as it was too far and out of their area.

Not to be deterred and knowing that the cat needed help, my husband and myself decided to drive to Wales one Sunday morning and when we were about half-way there, my husband said to me, 'Wait a minute, we are going all this way and how do we know that the cat will still be there when we arrive?' I then asked my guide and he told me that the cat would be asleep, under a tree, on the right hand side of the driveway leading up to the hotel. As we arrived and as predicted by my guide, the cat was sleeping at the base of the tree, on the right hand side as we drove in. Before he knew it, we had him safely in the basket and were back home by teatime – mission accomplished! We named him Thomas as he had come from Wales!

The next day, my husband took him to our local vets, where he received treatment for his mouth and eyes and was also neutered. On his return, he was placed in a separate pen in the cattery, as we mainly rescue mother cats and their kittens, and Thomas could not be allowed to mix with them in case a fight ensued! During this time in the cattery, we had a few feral mother cats with a number of kittens who were around five to eight weeks old and full of energy, so they were allowed to run free, including into the outside play area.

A few days later and to my husband's alarm, Thomas had somehow escaped from his pen. My husband quickly checked the outside run, only to find Thomas sitting with all of the ladies looking very content and pleased with himself, and very much in control of his harem! Thomas proved to be a true ladies man and in addition, he would play with the kittens and became a father figure to them all. Needless to say, Thomas was never penned up again! After a while, we allowed Thomas to roam freely and he joined in with our own cats. One day he went missing and after enquiries, my husband found Thomas up the road, on a neighbour's lap, enjoying a bowl of fish! Thomas endeared himself to everyone who met him and eventually found a loving home. Thomas truly paid us back for all the effort we made in rescuing him.

Whilst taking a demonstration of mediumship at a village hall in Essex, I had linked with an elderly lady and had communication for her from her husband in spirit. This gentleman proved to be a wonderful communicator, because of the close love that they had shared over many years of being together, and she was able to say 'Yes' to everything that I had given her, until the end of the message when I mentioned an Alsatian dog beside her from the world of spirit and she said, 'No, we never had a dog.' I then watched the dog walk along the front of the audience and stop beside a younger lady, who had her arms tightly crossed in front of her – as if to say 'Don't come to me!' I asked the lady if she could understand the Alsatian dog and she also said, 'No, I have never had an Alsatian dog.' I then said, 'Well, the dog's not moving, he is definitely with you. Wait a moment, let me describe him to you.' She then said, 'Yes, that's my Alsatian Collie Cross.' I then saw from spirit an older man come forward, who I felt was her grandfather and joined the dog. When I described him she replied, 'Yes, that is my grandfather.' I then became aware of a young boy building up in spirit, aged around nine years old and I said, 'I feel you've lost a son' and I described him to her and she said 'Yes, that is the son that I lost.' I said to the lady that they had come forward tonight to show that they were all together and safe in the world of spirit. This lady was so relieved to receive this information, which was all thanks to her dog who had taken me to her. Since then on a number of occasions an animal in spirit has taken me to their owner and this is often how my spirit communication starts.

I believe because of the animal work I have done over the years and the compassion and empathy I feel for all animals, I am allowed to see them in spirit. I always say that even a snail has an energy around it and that too goes into the spirit world. As previously stated, it is my belief that herd animals have a group soul and when you give love to just one of the group it then allows them to become an individual soul and helps with the animal's advancement. After all, I believe that this is why we are all here on the earth plane, to advance our spirit.

If animals could speak,
we wouldn't dare abuse them
– Taken from the book 'Wisdom Teachings'

Chapter Thirteen

Fred's Story

In the past, my husband was involved in the demolition and re-building of a property which had serious subsidence issues. The property was set in three quarters of an acre of grounds, surrounded by fields. The work started in early March and the property needed to be demolished first. Whilst one of the builders was using a Kango hammer to break up some concrete, he suddenly became aware of a beautiful male pheasant that was walking around him, totally undeterred by the noise and the builder decided to throw him a digestive biscuit. After that he was there every day looking for his digestive biscuit and the builders decided to name him Fred. Not the most appropriate name for such a good-looking bird! If you were too slow in producing the digestive biscuit he would follow you to the car and poke his head in – as if to say 'Where's my biscuit?!' As soon as they had erected some walls they created a tearoom, as builders can't work without their tea! Fred soon realised that there was a greater choice of food available in the tearoom and he would walk around the table taking food from the builders' hands.

When the weather started to warm up, Fred suddenly disappeared. For two weeks the builders could be heard calling for Fred but there was no sign of him. After two weeks, a great cheer went up from the builders, because there was Fred walking across the field with two female pheasants (one on either side of him). A shout went out from the builders, who found it very amusing, saying, 'Fred's a Jack the lad – he's pulled a couple of birds!' – and he had! Fred then came inside the fence, whilst the females stayed outside and collected some food to take back to them – a real gent! Fred only did this once, it was like he was saying to us, 'This is me and this is what I do.'

Fred then disappeared for a few weeks again and the builders were anxiously calling out and looking for him. Then one morning, across the field came Fred with one female and two chicks – a great cheer went out from the builders, with shouts of, 'Hooray, Fred's a family man!!' Fred only did this once, as once again he was showing us his lifestyle. Shortly after that Fred was with them every day. A few weeks later, my husband saw the builders lining up against the hedge and the language was turning slightly blue! My husband went over to see what all of the commotion was about and walking along the lane, outside the property, was a man carrying a shotgun and he was being suitably advised as to what would happen to him should a feather on Fred's head ever be harmed – they never saw him again! Fred had won the hearts and minds of the builders from the East End of London and they had become both his provider and protector.

When the property was sold, it was sold on condition that the new owners would look after Fred. Some eighteen months later, my husband met the new owners of the property in town and the first thing he asked them was, 'How's Fred, is he still enjoying his digestive biscuits?' 'No' they said, 'You've got to be joking, his dietary requirements have gone upmarket since then and when he wants his food he comes and taps on the patio doors!' Fred is truly one of the Creator's great creations.

How wonderful the world will be when animals are allowed to live with man and not be used for food or material gain – Taken from the book 'Wisdom Teachings'

Chapter Fourteen

The Hunters will be Hunted

Whilst taking a clairvoyant evening, I was taken by my guide to a gentleman in the audience and had made a connection with a close male relative of his in spirit. After giving details about him, the gentleman I had linked with fully understood who I had in the spirit world.

I was shown his relation sitting in a field, surrounded by rabbits. I then relayed to him what I had seen and he said that it didn't make any sense to him. Sadly, I was then shown a number of dead rabbits hanging up, having been shot. I then told him I was being shown his relation in spirit carrying a shot gun and that his relation used to shoot rabbits and did he understand this. The gentleman on the earth plane said that yes, he did.

I was then told by my guide that his relation was being made to sit in the field full of rabbits so he could learn about the lifestyle and social behaviour of these animals, and that he would need to remain there until he had learnt his lesson. I was given that due to his actions, in taking the life of these animals on his return to the earth plane he would be given the opportunity to correct the wrongs he had made previously, so he would know, deep in his sub-conscience, never to take the lives of animals again and hopefully this would be a life lesson learnt.

I believe that everything we do and all actions taken, good or bad, whilst living our earthly lives, are recorded in spirit and when we return home, we will judge ourselves, as all things will be stripped bare and we will see everything in a clear and crystal light, as we cannot hide from ourselves.

Animals have to fight for their existence against other animals but when they have to fight against man also, it's an impossibility
– Taken from the book 'Wisdom Teachings'

Chapter Fifteen

The Costa Blanca Feral Cat Trust

Whilst my parents were holidaying in Spain (in the early 1990s), my mother, Vera Davis, became aware of the plight of the street cats (ferals) and saw some that were dying, having been poisoned and others that had been drowned or discarded in rubbish bins. My mother vowed, there and then, that something would have to be done about the situation. Immediately, on my mother's return home, many animal charities, organisations and celebrities were contacted, some of whom had holiday homes in Spain but to no avail. Not to be discouraged, my dear mother went about starting her own charities. The first charity was called Cabo Roig & Torriveija Sanctuary, aptly named (CATS) but later the decision was made to hand it over to one of the original trustees, so that work could continue in that area, as my mother wanted to expand and cover other parts of the Costa Blanca to help as many cats as possible.

My mother then went on to form a second charity, called the Costa Blanca Feral Cat Trust, (CBFCT) and was the founder and chairperson. My mother's charity is registered with the Charities Commission in the UK and is also registered in Spain. My mother worked tirelessly to help the cats, setting up her own website and doing all of the organising and administration from the UK. Also, my mother would like to accompany everyone on their visits to Spain, to make sure that everything was as it should be and that it was all going to plan! My dear mother used to say, 'While I still have breath in my body, I will do everything I can to help the street cats.'

Once, or sometimes twice a year, my mother would organise flights from the UK and obtain accommodation in Spain, flying out a vet, vet nurses and trapper/drivers, to help the plight of the street cats. The ferals were then trapped, taken to the surgery, spayed or neutered, given pain relief, a multi-vitamin and flea and worming treatment. They would also receive a full health MOT and any other veterinary procedures that were required, including long acting antibiotics, had any infections been found. This often included treatment for eye or ear problems, any teeth that may have needed removal, cleaning of wounds etc. which could all be done whilst under the anaesthetic. Also, my mother would only ever use the best veterinary drugs, ordering them from the UK and then flying them out to Spain with her.

My dear mother's policy would always be 'To treat a feral cat in exactly the same way that you would a domestic cat'. All street cats have their left ears tipped (as agreed by the RSPCA International) for future identification, so as to prevent any further unnecessary sterilisations, as this can be dangerous. Generally, in just one week, around 200 cats were trapped and sterilised. After they had been operated on, the females would be left in overnight to recover and then checked in the morning before being re-released back to their original colonies. This procedure is known as Trap, Neuter & Return (TNR) and where possible, arrangements would be made to find feeders.

In the past, all of the family have been out to Spain to help the street cats. We originally started working in the town of Campello and the surrounding mountain villages. We then moved to the town of Calpe, where we are still working today, and so far approximately 2,000 street cats have been sterilised, but of course this number is added to every year. When my mother first went there, we were invited by the Mayor of Calpe, who had heard of my mother's compassionate work and was very pleased to have the CBFCT helping in his town, as he himself was in favour of a sterilisation programme, rather than the cats and kittens being disposed of by any cruel or inhumane means. Cats are still continuing to be trapped and brought in from nearby urbanisations and from as far away as Benidorm to the veterinary surgery in Calpe.

Visits were always advertised ahead in the local press, as to when the CBFCT would be coming to Calpe and local residents would contact us on arrival, who were in need of our help. Reports of our trips were often covered in the local paper, due to the interest that my mother's visits caused and once a local TV company filmed the vets operating on the cats in the surgery. A very kind German lady, who had her own programme of helping stray dogs in the town and re-homing them back in Germany, would let us use her villa and grounds as a temporary surgery. Sadly, there are very few shelters or homes in Spain but occasionally, before we flew back, we were sometimes fortunate enough to find homes for a few kittens.

Since the sad passing of my mother, Vera Davis, I have now become the Chairperson/Treasurer of the CBFCT, continuing to help with the funding of the cat sterilisation programme with my work as a public demonstration medium, and through the sales of my book, *Wisdom Teachings*, together with my bookmarks and CDs. We are fortunate enough to receive some funding from other charity organisations from time to time, which further helps us with the sterilisation of street cats. My daughter, Emma, is Secretary of the CBFCT, taking care of all of the administrative work and has also been to Spain trapping many times in the past. We also have an English trustee, who lives in Calpe and oversees the operations carried out in the surgery, by our Spanish vet, who is sympathetic to the need of the street cats.

My intention and hope is to continue helping to fund my mother's compassionate work, who in her seventies had the foresight, resolution and energy to start this in the first place, funds permitting.

A Further Note

Since the start of my Mother's amazing work in Calpe began, the Town Hall are now funding some sterilisations themselves, as they have seen not only the improvement in the health of the street cats, but also of their declining numbers.

My dear mother's compassionate and pioneering work really started something all those years ago. We are all so proud of her achievements and her legacy still lives on to this day.

'Bless everything that breathes
– we are the one breath'
– Taken from the book 'Wisdom Teachings'

Chapter Sixteen

Footsteps

Some years ago, my husband was involved in the restoration of an old small two bedroom cottage, dating back to 1875, at the end of a country lane leading to open fields. A truly beautiful location.

None of the old sash windows would open properly, so my father, Ron, being a builder, decorator and craftsman, was asked to renovate them. At the same time a team of builders were called in to assist with the rest of the renovation. During the early stages of the restoration, a tearoom was created in an upstairs bedroom, being the priority of the builders! Whilst they were having tea one day, they all heard footsteps crossing the floor downstairs. The builders rushed down to see who it was, only to find that there was no one there! This happened for three days running and sometimes there was the sound of the door opening first, which was an old door on a latch.

After the third occasion of this happening my husband, Terry, asked me to find out what was going on. I then asked my guide, Moo Chow Ching, for his guidance in this matter. He informed me that there were no problems, as it was only the elderly lady that had lived there for many years, coming back to see how the work was progressing. The elderly lady was interested in what was going on but was shy where men were concerned, so she would only visit when the men were upstairs having tea. It transpired, after enquiries with a neighbour, that the elderly lady had lived there for sixty years. Terry then told the builders of the information that I had received and they were quite happy with the explanation and were no longer worried when they heard the footsteps across the floor below!

As the work progressed, it came to the time when a new kitchen needed to be fitted. The kitchen fitter duly arrived and when it was time for a tea break he joined everyone in the tearoom upstairs. As was normal, when they were all upstairs the cottage door opened and the usual footsteps were heard crossing the floor below. None of the builders took any notice of this, having become used to the situation by now but the kitchen fitter, being concerned that someone had entered the cottage and with all of his tools downstairs, proceeded to rush down to see what was going on. Finding no one there he was quite shocked. Terry then informed him that it was only the spirit of the elderly lady who used to live there coming back to look at the progress and changes that had been made to her cottage. This alarmed the kitchen fitter so much that he was out of the door like a shot and went running down the lane, with Terry running after him saying, 'Stop! We need the kitchen fitted!' Fortunately, after a short while he calmed down, after the situation was fully explained to him. I am pleased to say that in due course the kitchen was finally finished!

If you are scared of something – look beyond it
– Taken from the book 'Wisdom Teachings'

CHAPTER SEVENTEEN

The Importance of Forgiveness

Several years ago, Terry and I went along to see a demonstration of clairvoyance at the Cliffs Pavillion, in Southend, Essex and the famous medium, Gordon Smith, was taking the evening. He worked by throwing out messages to the audience and in one message he said, 'I want to go to someone in the audience who knows someone who has just had, or is about to have, open heart surgery.' I then put my hand up and was handed the microphone and he asked me, 'Do you understand the name of George?' and I said, 'Yes, his name is George and he is about to undergo heart surgery in two days' time,' and he said, 'Then I am with you. I have his father here and he is telling me that he will survive the operation.' I then thanked him for his message, which had been very comforting and reassuring.

George was the name of my ex-husband and his father, who had communicated through Gordon Smith, had passed to spirit at the age of thirty one. George's father had been a wireless operator and tail gunner on Wellington bombers during the Second World War and at thirty one he was the oldest member of the crew. On returning from a raid over Germany, the plane was damaged by anti-aircraft fire and crashed over Holland, landing in Uden. Some of the crew had bailed out and survived but George's father stayed with the aircraft and managed to survive the crash landing. Sadly, as he made his way across a farmer's field he collapsed and died.

The following day, George's mother communicated with me from the world of spirit and confirmed to me also that her son would survive his imminent heart operation. Terry then asked me why his mother hadn't come through with his father at the time when Gordon Smith had given me the message. I then remembered in the past being told by George that at the time of his father's passing, his mother was no longer talking to her husband, because of an apparent indiscretion on his behalf and it appeared that she was still not communicating with him in the spirit world. I can only hope that with the passing of time there has now been a reconciliation between them.

I have linked many times with people from spirit who have connected with me purely for the sole purpose to ask their loved one, or friend for forgiveness and to say sorry and apologise to them for things they had done, or failed to do, whilst on the earth plane, as on their return to spirit they realised that they had to judge themselves and needed to put matters right before they were able to move on or make progress in spirit. Obviously, it is far better to put things right and resolve matters on the earth plane, as it will aid your progress on your return to spirit. Sadly, on some occasions, I have found that the person on the earth plane cannot bring themselves to forgive the person in spirit, which only prolongs the matter and therefore blocks both of those involved and as I understand it, unresolved differences can be taken to and continued on with in the world of spirit, so it is far better to reconcile your differences whilst on the earth plane, if possible.

In forgiving others – we forgive ourselves
– Taken from the book 'Wisdom Teachings'

Chapter Eighteen

The Guided Meditation Workshop

After the sad passing of my dear parents, I decided to close down my reflexology practice to be able to fully concentrate on my work as a public demonstration medium, especially as I was getting more and more recommendations to demonstrate in churches and other centres. I was given by my spirit guide, Moo Chow Ching, that I should be devoting more time to my mediumship, but closing down my practice was a hard step to take, as I had always loved giving treatments. It was a bit like stepping off a mountain, but I took the plunge and then fully concentrated on my work as a public demonstration medium.

Around this time, I was asked to take a guided meditation workshop. I have always done regular spiritual meditations, as I believe that this helps to lift your vibrations to a higher frequency, so that you can tune in more to the world of spirit, which exists on a higher, finer and less dense vibration. Learning to meditate can be hard at first, particularly when you are trying to calm the mind and concentrate on following the words of a guided meditation, as our mind tends to wander off. However, once mastered, it can be very beneficial to us on all levels. It can also relax you, clear the mind, allow spirit to harmonise and send healing to you and brings a wonderful sense of inner peace and calm. Of course, during meditation we can all send healing out to our loved ones, the world and the animal kingdom. It is well known that when healers send out healing thoughts at the same time, wonderful healing can take place. Also, of course it is when your guides, inspirers, helpers, healers and loved ones can draw close and communicate with you. I have often come back from a meditation with tears streaming down my face, especially when I have been thinking of my loved ones in the world of spirit.

After the guided meditation workshop, some of the group suggested to me that the meditations should be recorded. Easier said than done! This gave me food for thought, as I am always looking for ways to bring in monies to help fund the animal rescue that we do. It is wonderful how spirit can bring about help for you, especially at the right time. It so happened, that a gentleman who was attending the workshop (obviously pre-planned by spirit) had a relative that worked in the music business and also his own recording studio, and told me that he would contact him and ask if he would be able to help. It then came about that he was willing to help me and I went along with my husband to his recording studio in West London, complete with rock guitars in the foyer!

We spent the whole day at the studio and I managed to record two inspirationally guided meditations. The first CD was called *The Mansion*, where orchestral music leads you into a mansion house and takes you up the seven floors of the house, using the seven chakras, or energy centres, which correspond to the seven colours of the rainbow. Seven is a very spiritual number. After selling the first pressing of *The Mansion*, I then decided to bring out the second CD called *The Island*, which takes you on a lovely boat trip to an island, complete with atmospheric sounds and continues on a journey through the island and eventually leads you up to the top of a lighthouse. Both meditation CDs include how to 'open up' and 'close down' and Theta Wave Music to take you subliminally deeper and is especially aimed at those who wish to develop their spiritual gifts.

It is often necessary to be quiet
to get to the right answer
– Taken from the book 'Wisdom Teachings'

Chapter Nineteen

To the Edge and Back

In mid September 2015, I was at home with my husband and without warning, he suddenly went into a violent shivering fit and when he tried to get up he collapsed onto the floor, having lost the use of all of the muscles in his body. My husband asked me to ring his daughter, who works as an Advanced Nurse Practioner and as I described his symptoms, she said, 'Ring for an ambulance straight away, as Dad's got sepsis.' I quickly rang for an ambulance and when they arrived they rapidly assessed that he was in need of urgent medical attention. As my husband was put into the ambulance, I heard the ambulance driver radio ahead to say he was on the 'Blues and twos' and this one was 'straight for Resus'. I realised then that this must be serious. On arrival at Resus, there were a team of doctors and nurses waiting for him and they quickly diagnosed that he was suffering from sepsis. My husband's blood pressure had dropped and they were unable to raise it, despite all their efforts. Later that night he was admitted into Intensive Care and his situation became critical. My husband's condition continued to deteriorate and the sepsis started to attack every organ in his body and he was put on full life support and placed in a medically induced coma, to try to give his body the best chance to fight the infection. At 4am on the second morning, I received a call from the hospital to say that my husband's condition was critical and life-threatening and that his kidneys had failed and he was now on a kidney dialysis machine, so all of the family were informed.

By midday most of my husband's family and my daughter were with me in the family room, when the consultant and doctor came in and said the worst thing imaginable; that my husband had only two to three hours left to live. At this time he had gone into what is known as cold sepsis shock and his face and chest was turning blue/black. The family was then asked to come in, two at a time, to say their goodbyes. I thought that this cannot be happening. I went to a quiet place and my guide spoke to me in my mind and said that my husband would not be passing to the world of spirit and that he had gone to the edge, but was coming back and that he would come back stronger. My dear daughter also had a very strong belief that my husband would pull through this and was invaluable to me during this very difficult time, giving me a great amount of help and support.

I told the consultant I was a medium and that I was given from spirit that my husband wouldn't pass and that he would pull through and he obviously thought I was mad! I then went in to hold my husband's hand and gave him healing. About two hours later something remarkable happened, my husband's colour had returned and had changed from the awful blue/black, back to pink. I can only put this down to the incredible efforts and dedication of the medical team and the wonderful healing my husband was receiving, as all of the spiritual centres that we work at had been informed and my husband was put on all of their healing lists as well. Later that day, the consultant came back into the family room and said, 'Quite honestly what's happening here is nothing far short of a miracle.'

My husband spent nearly three weeks in Intensive Care, in a coma and altogether about two months in hospital. Also, during this time he lost two-and-a-half stone in weight, had a heart attack due to the strength of the drugs he was on, contracted one of the hospital super-bugs and had pneumonia.

Despite all this, my husband has made a full recovery and is no longer on any medication, as he had been before, and has in fact come back stronger as spirit had told me.

My dear guide, Moo Chow Ching, would give me constant daily updates on my husband's condition and what was happening. I cannot thank my guide enough for his constant communication and guidance during this critical time.

Sometimes you have to lift above the clouds
to where the sun is shining
– Taken from the book 'Wisdom Teachings'

Chapter Twenty

The Guides

As mentioned previously, our guides literally walk with us throughout our lives and are similar to ourselves and blend with our energies, but of course are on a more elevated level and vibration in the spirit world than we are on the earth plane. Our guides will inspire and guide us throughout our lives, especially when we allow them to connect with us, when sitting in a development circle or through meditation. I believe that we all have someone in spirit who is there for us, whether this is a loved one, helper or inspirer, especially when spirit become aware of us when we are linking with our higher selves, or sending out healing or working for the good of others.

Looking back, before I realised that I had a guide, I remember giving off guidance and wise words to people who needed help and thinking that it couldn't possibly be coming from me, as if I became a better me. This also happened on two or three occasions, where the person was so low that they wanted to end their own life. Of course, I now realise that my guide stepped in and took me over, or overshadowed me and helped by giving them some wonderful wisdom and guidance and so avoiding any tragic consequences.

As a guide, Moo Chow Ching has always been so kind, patient and wise in helping me to develop spiritually and has been a constant source of security, balance and a fountain of spiritual knowledge, giving me answers and guidance in so many areas of my life, especially during the challenging times. Of course, not all of my questions have been answered, as there are times when we have to go through something to learn and experience from it but when the time is right, we will always receive help.

Moo Chow Ching has always given me guidance through words, clairaudience (clear hearing), although as mentioned before, these words come as a thought pattern in my mind. Later on in my spiritual development, I have now added clairvoyance (clear seeing), to my work as a medium. Of course there is also clairsentience (clear sensing), which most mediums use as well, and indeed many of us in our everyday lives will also use this sense, as we often feel or sense certain things that we know to be right. A medium or healer is purely a channel to be used by the spirit world or higher divine energies.

It is wonderful when you become attuned to your guide, as of course they live on a much higher level or frequency to the earth plane and have to lower their vibration to connect and blend with your energy. The greatest thing is to learn to trust your guide and to trust in your own ability as to what you are receiving is correct and accurate. This can take a long time to achieve but once you have mastered this and have confidence in yourself, the connection that you obtain from spirit usually flows. Our earthly minds tend to go through doubts as to whether it is coming from us or our guide and of course this takes a lot of time and experience to learn and understand.

Having worked with Moo Chow Ching as my guide for many years and not liking change very much, a very disconcerting thing happened to me. I was half-way through a clairvoyant evening, when I noticed that I was receiving messages that weren't connected to the person that I was linking with, and then after a while I would go back to connecting correctly again. This happened to me on a few occasions and naturally it was quite worrying and had concerned me. I asked Moo Chow Ching as to what had caused the change in the way that I was working, and he told me that I had a new guide who wanted to work with me, and that I was being tuned into his vibration. Unfortunately, this needed to be done whilst I was working on the platform. Of course, tuning in can cause some disruption, rather like trying to tune into a new radio wave. Moo Chow Ching then told me that my new guide was his guide and that his name was Emperor Chan and he was also Chinese. A name is only important to us, as it helps us to connect with our guides, but in the higher levels of spirit, names are no longer necessary.

Later in meditations, I have seen Emperor Chan's palace in the spirit world and he always brings peacocks. I also understand that Emperor Chan had been waiting to see if I would continue along the spiritual pathway and as I had, he then allowed me to become his channel.

Although I am now working with Emperor Chan, I know that my first beloved guide, Moo Chow Ching continues to help, guide and support me and brings in philosophy and knowledge about the spirit world when I am working. Physically, I have also noticed the change that comes about when Emperor Chan is with me, as I have to drink quite a lot of water before I connect with spirit, as if it allows me to become a purer, clearer and more fluid channel. He also brings a great power in, rather like a turbo charge and gives me more energy with which to work. This whole process of change and alteration seems to have taken around two years to complete and of course the time in spirit is different to that on the earth plane. Before I work with Emperor Chan, I open up my chakras and reach up and tune into his energy. I then become aware of his presence and he takes control of the whole demonstration (which I now seem to be doing in a semi-trance like state). I then give off everything that I am receiving from spirit and this is in the form of a constantly flowing picture or video and become inspired to give what the spirit loved one, or loved ones wish to convey. Emperor Chan doesn't seem to use words but as I understand it, and have already mentioned before, in the higher levels of the spirit realms, words are no longer necessary.

When we work with spirit, we also have guides that are known as doorkeepers or gatekeepers. They are there to protect us and to control who is coming through from the world of spirit to work with us. We can also have other guides, helpers, inspirers, healers and loved ones who can assist when we are working. Also, other mediums that have passed to spirit may also wish to continue to work from their side of life to link with a medium on the earth plane to help with further proof of survival.

Our guides come from many different cultures and civilisations, some of which may be Native American, Oriental or Egyptian, to name but a few. They can also come from religious faiths, especially if their channel is of a higher mind. Interestingly, I know a medium who has a tramp as a guide and after taking a clairvoyant evening at her centre, I saw him appear in the doorway of the tearoom. I described him in detail and she fully accepted his description. My husband has a powerful Native American guide and protector and several mediums have confirmed this. He always felt protected in difficult and threatening situations during his time as a police officer.

Without our guides we would not be able to connect with spirit. I believe that some guides have lived an earthly life and that we may have met them before in a previous existence, as they would have experienced what life was like on earth.

I have also changed in the way that I work on the platform as a channel for spirit now, as all things should evolve. Whereas I used to see a projection from spirit, standing either behind or beside a person in the congregation or audience that I needed to link with, I will now usually see someone from spirit close to their energy and then the spirit person seems to stand in my aura, or energy field, where I feel I briefly become them, and I see or sense what they looked like and how they passed to spirit.

Sometimes, everything will just be within my mind (or psychic eye) and I can work from here. Spirit usually take me to the person directly that I need to link with but on some occasions, they may just be in my aura and I will need to give the evidence out to the audience. I am learning to be more adaptable! I used to perhaps receive one spirit communication per person but more recently, I may have two or three spirit connections that come in and sometimes a beloved bird or animal may accompany them, as all life goes on from this world to the next. Sometimes spirit will still project as well, (the way I used to work) and I am also aware that spirit see the light of the medium on the earth plane and then want to work in their channel. I usually see this as a beacon of light and often liken it to being at an airport with many planes circulating above and then slotting in when the time is right for spirit to communicate. Also, the spirit presence will have to lower their vibrations from the spirit world in order to link in with the slower vibrations of the earth plane. The earth plane exists on a very heavy and dense vibration (matter), whereas the spirit world varies in the lightness of frequency, as you ascend to higher levels, where the vibration would become higher, lighter and faster.

Often, as mediums develop, they can in their lifetime have several different guides or influences that have worked with them, during each stage of their development. I also have a French Sister of Mercy, that brings healing and calm when I work.

Also, those that have loved us can continue to help from spirit. I know that my dear father also connects with me when I work, especially as he was so spiritually aware and I sense that he has now advanced to guide level in the world of spirit. Of course, those that work with healing also channel spirit through their healing guides. I always say when I work that I could never do this without the guides, as they are the control and the medium is purely an instrument for spirit to use. I often see this as working with an orchestra with the guides and those around us in spirit, each having their role to play.

Before taking a demonstration of clairvoyance or a church service, I like to prepare and adjust (to working in an altered state of consciousness). I always ask for a cloak of protection to be placed around me and then call in all of the guides, although Emperor Chan controls everything. As previously stated, I also open up the seven chakras, or energy centres that lie within the physical body. More recently, I have also been opening some extra chakras, four of which are placed outside the physical body. When I finish working with spirit, I always close my chakras down. The spirit world do not live on the earth's heavy vibrations and come in from a much higher frequency, that is to say the light, as this is where your loved ones live.

I believe that before we come back to the earth plane, our guides have chosen to work with us and of course sincerely hope that we will stay on our pathway and achieve our soul's purpose, thereby adhering to our life's plan.

I would like to add here that we can all ask for a cloak of protection to be placed around us, whether we are working spiritually or not, especially if we ever find ourselves in a situation where we may need some protection. I also find this helpful before commencing a journey. You can visualise this as a cloak placed around yourself and enclosing you, or imagine a beautiful white light surrounding you. Another strong protector is to see yourself in a pyramid. This can be a light pyramid with glass walls, as a pyramid is made up of three sections and three is a very spiritual number. It represents the Father, Son and Holy Spirit and of course, mind, body and spirit.

We need someone better to teach us
– Taken from the book 'Wisdom Teachings'

Chapter Twenty One

Past Lives

One day, during a meditation, my guide told me that in my previous life, I had lived as a French Sister of Mercy, and that the convent was close to the French/Italian border. It later made sense to me, when I discovered that I have a French Sister of Mercy who also works with me, and whose name is Celestine, whom I would have known from my time in the convent. I was also told by my guide, that during the same period my husband, Terry, had lived a life as a monk in the nearby monastery and we had met briefly, but obviously couldn't marry!

My guide also informed me that my daughter, Emma, had lived a life as a nurse in the First World War, which may explain why she is so caring and has a lot of medical knowledge in this life (although she has a completely different profession this time round). My daughter shows so much empathy and care, when family or friends are unwell and indeed was brilliant with her father when he needed nursing and has been there at hospital bedsides many times when friends or loved ones have been seriously ill, or passing to spirit. Interestingly, even the name of Emma means nurse.

It is my belief that the soul evolves through many lives, as we cannot learn and experience all of life's lessons in just one lifetime, as whatever we have done wrong, or mistakes we have made in a previous life, will need to be corrected in order to balance the books of life (known as Karmic Law). I always say that the earth plane is a school of learning. I also believe that we elect to go through certain experiences and know the plans that are ahead of us whilst in spirit, but we are normally not allowed to bring this knowledge back with us.

My husband is also a great believer in past lives, as he has a vivid memory of his parents taking him to the town of Taunton, in Somerset, when he was about eight years of age. He recalls walking along a street and just before turning right, he knew he would see three important buildings and as he turned the corner, there in front of him, were the three buildings that he knew would be there, although he had never been to Taunton before. Well not in this life anyway! So my husband feels that he has lived in that area before in a past life.

As said previously, we sometimes return to put right wrongs, from a previous life and often come back with memories that are buried deep within our sub-conscious mind, as to what occurred in another life. We can return with an unexplained fear, of which there is no apparent, rational explanation. I believe that the more lives we have lived, we instinctively know that we have lived before. It is only when we have reached and attained a certain advancement in our evolution, we will be allowed to remain in spirit and not have to return to the earth plane, because we would have learnt and experienced all of the lessons that we were meant to have learnt. As I understand it, under normal circumstances, we are not allowed to have knowledge of why we are here.

The following stories are just a few examples of how past life experiences can manifest themselves in this life.

Going back to when I was a reflexologist, a lady came to me for treatment but had no interest in mediumship whatsoever. Whilst receiving treatment, my guide told me that she had an unexplained fear of water and that I was allowed to tell her the reason why, and it was because she had drowned in a previous life. When I told her this, she replied, 'I have always had this fear of water but couldn't understand why.' Having this explained to her gave her some understanding of why she had this unexplained fear.

On another occasion, I was giving treatment to a lady, who had come to see if she could receive help with a long term lung condition that she had been suffering from. At the end of the session, she felt that a great weight had been lifted from her and she could breathe more freely. I was told by my guide that she was very fearful of passing away with this condition and felt that she would only have a short life. I was then given by my guide that the lady had passed to spirit in a past life at a similar age with the same condition and that she had brought this deep seated memory back with her, but would not have a short life in this existence. I then relayed to her this privileged information and she accepted what my guide had told me, as it made absolute sense to her. Everything is controlled by spirit and happens at the correct time and for this lady, it was obviously the right time of releasing her past condition, as her health continued to improve.

Another time, when I was nearing the end of a reading I was giving to a lady, I was shown by my guide that she had been trapped alive in a cave and she sadly passed away in there. As I gave this information to her, she confirmed she had experienced this recurring image throughout her life and also that this was further confirmed during a session of past life regression.

Another example was when I was linking with a lady whom I was shown had lived a life as a young boy on a ship and one day, whilst climbing up the rigging on the mast, slipped and tragically fell, losing his life. This lady accepted what spirit had given her, as she had also been told this previously when she had been for some past life regression.

I also remember a lady who had a great fear of water and I was told by my guide that she had drowned in a past life, which caused her to have a feeling of pressure on her lungs and a tightness of breath. When I told her this, she was relieved to have an explanation as to why she had been experiencing this. When an answer is given from spirit, it brings great relief to the person and then allows the healing process to take place.

One evening in circle, whilst having a conversation with one of our members, he mentioned that he had a paranoid fear of rats and just the sight and thought of one would send him into shivers of fear. Immediately, I realised that this was due to a past life situation. As I connected with spirit on a deeper level, I was shown that in a previous life he had been chained to a wall in a dungeon and had been attacked by rats and there was no way of escaping from this horrendous situation. No wonder he had a fear of rats!

These stories are an example of some of the deep seated fears that can be brought back with us from previous existences, but in general we don't have the answers as to why we have these deep seated fears and anxieties, as very few of us will ever know the answers until we return to spirit, where all things will be made clear to us.

I remember hearing the story of a young woman who had lived a terrible life, having been in care and had experienced many other problems and in her early thirties, her existence became so unbearable that she decided to end her life. However, she didn't quite succeed, which resulted in her having a near death experience, where she described arriving in the world of spirit, only to be made instantly aware of why her life had been so hard. Immediately, she recalled apologising and on returning to the earth plane she was able to continue her life with the clear understanding as to why her existence had been so difficult previously. This is a rare example of someone being given knowledge of a previous existence.

As mentioned before, some people return to this life to right wrongs from an earlier existence. I believe that in most cases, while we are back home in spirit, we are able to elect which situation and life we would choose to live, so as to give us the best opportunity to correct the previous wrongs. I also believe that some will have no choice as to what their next life should be, if for instance they had previously harmed people or animals, spirit would automatically place them into a life from which they would have deep learning and depending on how severe their harm was, this could take many lives of learning to clear their Karmic Law. On the other hand, I absolutely believe that some advanced souls do elect to re-incarnate onto the earth plane, to help with the progress of mankind.

One example of righting wrongs is of a boy who at a young age developed epilepsy. Various treatments were tried without success and tragically, in his late twenties and due to the fact he felt he had no quality of life left, he decided to take his own life. During a meeting with his father, I was told by spirit that in his previous life on earth, his son had been a member of the SS, during the Second World War and had been shot in the head. As soon as I told his father this, he looked visibly shaken and said, 'When his son was born he had an indentation in his skull.' I was then given that on his son's return to spirit, after taking his own life, he was not being punished any further, due to the fact he had already suffered enough. I was then shown his son in spirit sitting under a tree, where he was painting. His father then told me that this was one of his son's favourite hobbies. I also believe that you can continue on in spirit using the gifts that you had whilst on the earth plane. On other occasions, I have met a few people with either a scar or birthmark in the same position on their body, where an injury or something similar had happened to them, in a previous life.

I believe that we come back in soul groups, as many of us, when meeting someone for the first time, can feel an immediate and unexplained connection with them and are on the same wavelength. Often, someone who is a mother in this life, could have been the daughter or sister before, or the father could have been the son or brother in a previous life, and many of us feel and know when we meet up with a soulmate.

Living many lives may make some sense as to why some people only have short lives, as this could be due to needing to finish something left undone from their previous life, and this would only require a shorter period of time to complete. Also, if in a past life we had attained a great amount of knowledge or expertise in a certain subject, this could be an explanation as to why some children become exceptionally gifted at an early age.

Of course, the more lives we have lived in different countries with other faiths, will eventually give us more empathy and understanding of others. I believe we are the sum total of all of the lives that we have led before.

We will keep coming back until we get it right
– Taken from the book 'Wisdom Teachings'

CHAPTER TWENTY TWO

A Foot in Both Worlds

A very unusual thing happened to me in the past, when a lady came to me for reflexology. While she was with me, I became aware of a gentleman in spirit with her. I described him in detail and also his character but I did not feel he was a family member. Instantly, she recognised him as a very good friend of hers, who she had known for many years. The lady looked quite startled and told me that he was still alive. Apparently, he had been a wonderful healer and had been in a coma for about a year. I then said, 'Well, I have him here and he is communicating with me from the spirit world,' which was of course very puzzling to me at the time. It was then explained to me by my guide, that although his body was still here on the earth plane, spirit had been kind and freed him from the confines of his physical body, because of all of the unconditional healing and help he had given to others.

I know the account of how this happened sounds very strange but this is exactly how it was. Since then, on very rare occasions, the same type of scenario has occurred and in each case it has proved that at that precise moment in time, the person on the earth plane had been very seriously ill.

On another occasion, I remember taking an evening of clairvoyance, where I was linking in with a lady, whose father had connected with me in detail, with all of the evidence being accepted. I then felt another spirit presence, whom I identified as being her mother, and said to the lady that I felt that her mother had had a problem with her mind. Although the lady could accept everything I had given to her, she couldn't understand what was happening, as her mother was still living. I said to her, 'Could you accept that your mother is seriously ill?' The lady replied, 'Yes, she is suffering from a serious case of dementia.' I then said to the lady, 'Can you also accept that your mother is talking to your father?' The lady smiled and said, 'Yes, she is talking to my father everyday, as she is living with me and I hear her talking to him.' I then went on to explain to her about her mother actually being with him in the world of spirit, even though her physical body was still on the earth plane. It appeared that her mother had a foot in both worlds at the same time. It appears the spirit can be free, even if the body is trapped.

I always say that we are spirit in a body now, which may explain a little of what happened when I was communicating with spirit.

Death is of the body but not of the spirit
– Taken from the book 'Wisdom Teachings'

Chapter Twenty Three

In Conclusion

Looking back to when I had my first out of body experience, around the age of eleven (and having previously lived a life as a nun in a cloistered existence), could explain why I had a fear of open spaces and the need to be in a safe and known environment. It is interesting to think that my work as a public demonstration medium now sees me standing up in front of an audience, with no place to run or hide! How life can change and I still wonder sometimes, how I can do it!

Interestingly, the story so far has taken us to work at the beautiful church, The London Spiritual Mission (LSM) in Bayswater, West London, which has been graced by many famous mediums over the years, the latest being Gordon Smith, who is now also the president of the LSM. It is strange how life has come back to an almost full circle, as Bayswater was where my dear ballet teacher, Miss S once lived. Miss Spalding used to shop at Whiteleys, which was a well-known local department store and the LSM was once used by Whiteleys as their stables, so when I go there it not only connects me with the past but also with the here and now.

It is my belief that proof of survival covers all beliefs and should not be in conflict with any religion. What I, or any other medium is trying to prove, is that we survive beyond this world and into the next. Many times I have linked in with people of different faiths, as they were anxious to find out if their loved ones had survived, and hopefully I have been able to prove this. I believe that love is the greatest power of all, and that loved ones in the world of spirit have a need and desire to communicate with us, to let us know that they are safe and well and living on in the world of spirit.

It is also my understanding that if we have lived with a strong religious faith, we will return to an area of spirit where there are like minded souls and where we would feel most comfortable. With the passage of time, however, we will realise that 'we are all one' and should not be divided by any religious faiths or beliefs and we should live in harmony with one another.

We cannot die, as life continues from this world and into the next, because we are energy and energy just transforms and transfers itself into another state of being. There is continuity of life from this life to the next. Life after life. I believe our minds, or consciousness and the love and emotion in our hearts, is what we take with us into the world of spirit. There will also be records kept of how we have lived our lives, whilst on the earth plane.

Of course, there are some people, who have no belief in life after death and when communicating with them, after they have passed to the spirit world, they will often come through to say that they never had any belief in the afterlife at all whilst on the earth plane, but of course their views have changed now, but even this acknowledgement can take time for them to accept and adjust to.

On a personal note and one that is very dear to my heart, I would like to quote something that my compassionate and inspirational guide, Moo Chow

Ching has told me, which is, 'While mankind continues to persecute and eat the animals, there will never be peace on the earth plane', which is something that I whole-heartedly agree with. Surely the animals have the right to their own existence and in treating the animals with the respect they deserve, we will be advancing, not only them but ourselves as well.

There is no need for the majority of us to eat meat anymore, as nowadays such a wide variety of food is plentifully available, which is better for us and of course the planet, and I believe that this is now the way forward. I always send my prayers to ask for help for all of those farm animals, throughout the world, that have to go to their deaths every day and whose lives have been ended so abruptly and prematurely. They have no voice in which to speak for themselves and they experience the same fear and pain as we do. May I leave these thoughts with you in the hope of a kinder and more compassionate world in the future. I always say that the world starts with us, so let us hope that each and every one of us can, and will, make the world a better place.

This book has been written in love for both people and animals and it is my hope that it may answer a few of your spiritual questions and shed some light as to why we are here.

Finally, I would like to leave you with one of my dear father's wise sayings – *'If you cease to strive – you cease to live.'* May I wish you all well on your life's journey.

> *The end is just the beginning*
> *– Taken from the book 'Wisdom Teachings'*

And the journey continues...

61054